CONTENTS

ASIAN MARINADE — 1

Yield: Approximately 1¼ cups

INGREDIENTS:

- ¼ cup fish sauce
- ¼ cup soy sauce (if possible low-sodium)
- ½ cup freshly squeezed lime juice
- 1 tablespoon curry powder
- 1 tablespoon light brown sugar
- 1 teaspoon minced garlic Crushed dried red pepper
- 2 tablespoons crispy peanut butter

DIRECTIONS:

1. Mix all the ingredients in a blender or food processor and pulse until the desired smoothness is achieved.

ASIAN MARINADE — 2

Yield: Approximately 1¼ cups

INGREDIENTS:

- ¼ cup chopped green onion
- ¼ cup soy sauce
- ¼ teaspoon ground anise
- ½ cup lime juice
- 1 tablespoon freshly grated gingerroot
- 1 tablespoon honey
- 1 teaspoon Chinese 5-spice powder
- 2 tablespoons hoisin sauce
- 2 tablespoons sesame oil
- 3 cloves garlic, minced
- 3 tablespoons chopped cilantro
- 1 cup vegetable oil

DIRECTIONS:

1. Mix the lime juice, soy sauce, hoisin sauce, and honey, and blend thoroughly.
2. Slowly whisk in the vegetable and sesame oils. Put in the rest of the ingredients and mix meticulously.

BLACK BEAN PASTE

Yield: Approximately ½ cup

INGREDIENTS:

- 1 medium to big onion, minced
- 1 tablespoon fish sauce
- 1 teaspoon brown sugar
- 2 cloves garlic, chopped
- 2 jalapeños, seeded and chopped
- 2 tablespoons vegetable oil
- 2 teaspoons lime juice
- 3 green onions, trimmed and cut
- 4 tablespoons canned black beans or black soy beans

DIRECTIONS:

1. In a moderate-sized-sized sauté pan, heat the oil over moderate-the onions, jalapeños, garlic, and green onions, and sauté onion becomes translucent.
2. Using a slotted spoon, move the sautéed vegetables to processor or blender (set aside the oil in the sauté pan). rest of the ingredients and process for a short period of time to create a not-paste.
3. Reheat the reserved oil in the sauté pan. Move the paste and heat for five minutes, stirring continuously. If the paste seems thick, add a small amount of water.

CHILI TAMARIND PASTE

Yield: Approximately 3 cups

INGREDIENTS:

- ½ cup dried shrimp
- 1 cup cut shallots
- 1 tablespoon fish sauce
- 1¾ cups vegetable oil, divided
- 12 small Thai chilies or
- 3 tablespoons brown sugar
- 3 tablespoons Tamarind Concentrate (Page 20)

- 6 serrano chilies
- 1 cup garlic

DIRECTIONS:

1. Put the dried shrimp in a small container. Cover the shrimp stir for a short period of time, and drain; set aside.
2. Pour 1½ cups of the vegetable oil in a moderate-sized deep cooking pan. the oil to roughly 360 degrees on moderate to high heat.
3. Put in the garlic and fry until a golden-brown colour is achieved. Using a slotted move the garlic to a container lined using paper towels.
4. Put in the shallots to the deep cooking pan and fry for two to three minutes; the shallots to the container with the garlic.
5. Fry the reserved shrimp in the deep cooking pan for a couple of minutes; the container.
6. Fry the chilies until they become brittle, approximately half a minute; them to the container. (Allow oil to cool completely discarding.)
7. Mix the fried ingredients, the rest of the oil, and the a food processor; process to make a smooth paste.
8. Put the paste in a small deep cooking pan on moderate heat. Put in the sugar and fish sauce, and cook, stirring once in a while, for approximately five minutes.
9. Allow the paste to return to room temperature before placing in an airtight container.

CHILI VINEGAR

Yield: Approximately ½ cup

INGREDIENTS:

- ½ cup white vinegar
- 2 teaspoons fish sauce
- 3 serrano chilies, seeded and finely cut

DIRECTIONS:

1. Put all of the ingredients in a container.
2. Allow to sit minimum twenty minutes to allow the flavors to develop.

COCONUT MARINADE

Yield: Approximately ½ cup

INGREDIENTS:

- ¼–½ teaspoon red chili pepper flakes
- 1 tablespoon grated lime zest
- 1 tablespoon minced fresh ginger
- 2 tablespoons shredded, unsweetened coconut
- 2 teaspoons sugar
- 3 tablespoons lime juice
- 3 tablespoons rice wine vinegar
- teaspoon curry powder

DIRECTIONS:

1. Warm the vinegar using low heat. Put in the coconut and ginger to become tender.
2. Turn off the heat and mix in the rest of the ingredients.

GREEN CURRY PASTE — 1

Yield: 1 cup

INGREDIENTS:

- ¼ cup vegetable oil
- ½ cup chopped cilantro
- ½ teaspoon ground cloves
- ½ teaspoon shrimp paste
- 1 (1½-inch) piece gingerroot, peeled and chopped
- 1 stalk lemongrass, tough outer leaves removed, inner soft portion chopped
- 1 teaspoon black pepper
- 1 teaspoon ground cumin
- 1 teaspoon salt
- 10 green serrano chilies
- 2 teaspoons grated lime zest
- 2 teaspoons ground coriander
- 2 teaspoons ground nutmeg
- 3 shallots, crudely chopped
- 5 cloves garlic

DIRECTIONS:

1. Put the first 6 ingredients in a food processor and process mixed. Put in the rest of the ingredients, apart from the vegetable process until the desired smoothness is achieved.
2. Slowly put in the oil until a thick paste May be placed in the fridge up to 4 weeks.

GREEN CURRY PASTE — 2

Yield: Approximately 1 cup

INGREDIENTS:

- 1 (1-inch) piece ginger, peeled and chopped
- 1 medium onion, chopped
- 1 teaspoon salt
- 1 teaspoon shrimp paste
- 2 green bell peppers, seeded and chopped
- 2 tablespoons vegetable oil
- 2 teaspoons chopped lemongrass
- 2 teaspoons cumin seeds, toasted
- 2–4 green jalapeño chilies, seeded and chopped
- 3 cloves garlic, chopped
- 3 tablespoons coriander seeds, toasted
- 3 teaspoons water
- 4 tablespoons chopped cilantro
- 4 tablespoons Tamarind Concentrate (Page 20)

DIRECTIONS:

1. Put all the ingredients in a food processor and pulse until the desired smoothness is achieved. Move to a small deep cooking pan and bring to a simmer on moderate to low heat. Decrease the heat to low and cook, stirring regularly, for five minutes.
2. Mix in 1 cup of water and bring the mixture to its boiling point. Decrease the heat, cover, and simmer for half an hour

LEMON CHILI VINEGAR

INGREDIENTS:

- 1 quart white wine vinegar Peel of 4 limes
- 8–10 serrano chilies

DIRECTIONS:

1. Mix all the ingredients in a moderate-sized deep cooking pan and bring to a simmer on moderate heat.
2. Decrease the heat and simmer for about ten minutes.
3. Cool to room temperature, then strain.

Yield: Approximately 1 quart

LEMONGRASS MARINADE

Yield: Approximately 1 cups

INGREDIENTS:

- ¼ tablespoon soy sauce
- 1 cup extra-virgin olive oil
- 1 jalapeño chili pepper, seeded and chopped
- 1 tablespoon fish sauce
- 2 cloves garlic, minced
- 2 stalks lemongrass, trimmed and smashed
- 2 tablespoons chopped cilantro
- 2 tablespoons lime juice

DIRECTIONS:

1. Pour the olive oil into a pan and heat until warm.
2. Put in the lemongrass and garlic, and cook for a minute. Turn off the heat and let cool completely.
3. Mix in the rest of the ingredients.

MALAYSIAN MARINADE

Yield: Approximately 1 cup

INGREDIENTS:

- ¼ cup chopped cilantro
- ¼ cup soy sauce
- ¼ cup vegetable oil

- ½ teaspoon coriander
- ½ teaspoon ground cumin
- 1 green onion, trimmed and thinly cut
- 1 teaspoon grated lime zest
- 2 tablespoons grated gingerroot
- 2 tablespoons honey
- 3 tablespoons lime juice

DIRECTIONS:

1. Mix the honey, lime juice, lime zest, and soy sauce in a small container.
2. Slowly whisk in the oil.
3. Mix in the rest of the ingredients.

MINTY TAMARIND PASTE

Yield: Approximately 2 cups

INGREDIENTS:

- ¼ cup peanuts
- ½ cup Tamarind Concentrate (Page 20)
- 1 bunch cilantro leaves
- 1 bunch mint leaves
- 4–5 Thai bird peppers or 2 serrano chilies, seeded and chopped

DIRECTIONS:

1. Put all the ingredients in a food processor and pulse to make a paste.

NORTHERN (OR JUNGLE) CURRY PASTE

Yield: Approximately 2 cups

INGREDIENTS:

- ¼ cup chopped arugula
- ¼ cup chopped chives
- ½ cup chopped mint
- 1 (3-inch) piece ginger, peeled and chopped
- 1 cup chopped basil
- 1 stalk lemongrass, tough outer leaves removed and discarded, inner core minced

- 1 tablespoon shrimp paste
- 12 serrano chilies, seeded and chopped
- 2 tablespoons vegetable oil
- 4 shallots, chopped
- 6–8 Thai bird chilies, seeded and chopped

DIRECTIONS:

1. In a moderate-sized-sized sauté pan, heat the oil on medium. Put in shrimp paste, lemongrass, ginger, and shallots, and sauté until shallots start to turn translucent and the mixture is very aromatic.
2. Move the mixture to a food processor and pulse until adding 1 or 2 tablespoons of water to help with the grinding.
3. Put in the rest of the ingredients and more water if required to pulse until crudely mixed.

RED CURRY PASTE— 1

Yield: Approximately ½ cup

INGREDIENTS:

- 1 (½-inch) piece ginger, finely chopped
- 1 medium onion, chopped
- 1 stalk lemongrass, outer leaves removed and discarded, inner core finely chopped
- 1 teaspoon salt
- 2 garlic cloves, chopped
- 2 tablespoons Tamarind Concentrate (Page 20)
- 2 teaspoons cumin seeds, toasted
- 2 teaspoons paprika
- 3 kaffir lime leaves or the peel of 1 lime, chopped
- 3 tablespoons coriander seeds, toasted
- 3 tablespoons vegetable oil
- 4 tablespoons water
- 6–8 red serrano chilies, seeded and chopped

DIRECTIONS:

1. Put all the ingredients in a food processor and pulse until super smooth.
2. Move to a small deep cooking pan and bring to a simmer on moderate to low heat. Decrease the heat to low and cook, stirring regularly, for five minutes.
3. Mix in 1 cup of water and bring the mixture to its boiling point. Decrease the heat, cover, and simmer thirty minutes.

Yield: Approximately 1 cup

INGREDIENTS:

- 1 (2-inch) piece ginger, peeled and thoroughly minced
- 1 small onion, chopped
- 2 cloves garlic, minced
- 2 stalks lemongrass, tough outer leaves removed and discarded, inner core thoroughly minced
- 2 tablespoons ground turmeric
- 3 big dried red California chilies, seeded and chopped
- 5 dried Thai bird or similar chilies, seeded and chopped

DIRECTIONS:

1. Put the chilies in a container and cover them with hot water. Allow to stand for minimum 30 minutes. Drain the chilies, saving for later 1 cup of the soaking liquid.
2. Put all the ingredients and 2–3 tablespoons of the soaking liquid in a food processor. Process to make a thick, smooth paste. Put in additional liquid if required.

SHREDDED FRESH COCONUT

Yield: Approximately 1 cup

INGREDIENTS:

- 1 heavy coconut, with liquid

DIRECTIONS:

1. Preheat your oven to 400 degrees.
2. Pierce the eye of the coconut using a metal skewer or screwdriver and drain the coconut water (reserve it for later use if you prefer).
3. Bake the coconut for fifteen minutes, then remove and allow to cool.
4. When the coconut is sufficiently cool to handle, use a hammer to break the shell. Using the tip of a knife, cautiously pull the flesh from the shell. Remove any remaining brown membrane with a vegetable peeler.
5. Shred the coconut using a 4-sided grater. Fresh coconut will keep in your fridge for maximum one week.

SOUTHERN (OR MASSAMAN) CURRY PASTE

Yield: Approximately 1 cup

INGREDIENTS:

- ¼ teaspoon ground cinnamon
- ¼ teaspoon whole black peppercorns
- ½ teaspoon cardamom seeds, toasted
- 1 (1-inch) piece ginger, peeled and minced
- 1 stalk lemongrass, tough outer leaves removed and discarded, inner core finely chopped
- 1 teaspoon lime peel
- 1 teaspoon salt
- 1 teaspoon shrimp paste (not necessary)
- 2 tablespoons coriander seeds, toasted
- 2 tablespoons vegetable oil
- 2 teaspoons brown sugar
- 2 teaspoons cumin seeds, toasted
- 2 whole cloves
- 3 tablespoons Tamarind Concentrate (Page 20)
- 3 tablespoons water
- 6–8 big dried red chilies (often called California chilies), soaked in hot water for five minutes and drained

DIRECTIONS:

1. Put all ingredients in a food processor and pulse until the desired smoothness is achieved.
2. Move to a small deep cooking pan and bring to a simmer on moderate to low heat. Decrease the heat to low and cook, stirring regularly, for five minutes.
3. Mix in 1 cup of water and bring the mixture to its boiling point. Decrease the heat, cover, and simmer thirty minutes.

TAMARIND CONCENTRATE

Yield: Approximately 1 cup

INGREDIENTS:

- 1 cup warm water
- 2 ounces seedless tamarind pulp (sold in Asian markets)

DIRECTIONS:

1. Put the tamarind pulp and water in a small container for about twenty minutes or until the pulp is tender.
2. Break the pulp apart using the backside of a spoon and stir until blended.
3. Pour the mixture through a fine-mesh sieve, pushing the tender pulp through the strainer. Discard any fibrous pulp remaining in the strainer.

TAMARIND MARINADE

Yield: Approximately 2 cups

INGREDIENTS:

- ¼ cup fresh lime juice
- ¼ cup toasted, unsweetened coconut
- ¼ cup vegetable oil
- ½ cup chopped cilantro leaves
- 1 shallot, chopped
- 1 tablespoon brown sugar
- 1 tablespoon diced fresh gingerroot
- 1 tablespoon soy sauce
- 1½ cups Tamarind Concentrate (Page 20)
- 2 garlic cloves, minced
- 4 pieces lime peel (roughly ½-inch by two-inches)

DIRECTIONS:

1. Mix the tamarind and lime peel in a small deep cooking pan and bring to a simmer; cook for five minutes.
2. Turn off the heat and cool completely. Mix in the rest of the ingredients.

THAI GRILLING RUB

Yield: Approximately

INGREDIENTS:

- 1 teaspoon dried lime peel
- 1 teaspoon freshly ground black pepper
- 1 teaspoon ground ginger
- 4 teaspoons salt

DIRECTIONS:

1. Mix all the ingredients and mix meticulously. Store in an airtight container.
2. To use, wash the meat of your choice under cool water and pat dry; drizzle the meat with the spice mixture (to taste) and rub it in together with some olive oil, then grill or broil to your preference.

THAI MARINADE — 1

Yield: Approximately 1 cup

INGREDIENTS:

- ¼ cup chopped cilantro
- ¼ cup fresh lime juice
- ¼ teaspoon hot pepper flakes
- ½ cup sesame oil
- 1 big stalk lemongrass, crushed
- 1 tablespoon brown sugar
- 2 tablespoons chopped peanuts
- 2 tablespoons fish sauce
- 3 cloves garlic, minced

DIRECTIONS:

1. Mix the fish sauce and lime juice in a small container.
2. Slowly whisk in the sesame oil, then mix in rest of the ingredients.

THAI MARINADE — 2

Yield: Approximately 1½ cups

INGREDIENTS:

- ¼ cup chopped basil leaves
- ¼ cup chopped mint leaves
- ¼ cup peanut oil
- ½ cup rice wine

- 1 small onion, chopped
- 1 tablespoon chopped gingerroot
- 1 tablespoon sweet soy sauce
- 2 tablespoons chopped lemongrass
- 3 cloves garlic, minced
- 3 tablespoons fish sauce

DIRECTIONS:

1. Mix the fish sauce, sweet soy sauce, and the rice wine in a small container.
2. Slowly whisk in the peanut oil, then mix in rest of the ingredients.

THAI MARINADE — 3

Yield: Approximately 2 cups

INGREDIENTS:

- ¼ cup chopped cilantro leaves
- ¼ cup lime juice
- ½ cup Red Curry Paste (Page 17)
- 1 (12-ounce) can coconut milk
- 1 stalk lemongrass, roughly chopped
- 1 tablespoon sweet soy sauce
- 1 teaspoon fresh gingerroot, chopped
- 2 tablespoons fish sauce
- 6 kaffir lime leaves, finely cut

DIRECTIONS:

1. Mix the coconut milk, curry paste, lemongrass, and kaffir leaves in a small deep cooking pan; bring to a simmer on moderate heat.
2. Decrease the heat and carry on simmering for fifteen minutes.
3. Turn off the heat and let cool to room temperature.
4. Mix in all the rest of the ingredients.

THAI VINEGAR MARINADE

Yield: Approximately 3 cups

INGREDIENTS:

- ¼ cup chopped lemongrass
- 1 tablespoon fresh grated gingerroot
- 1 tablespoon sugar
- 2–3 tablespoons vegetable oil
- 3 tablespoons chopped green onion
- 3½ cups rice wine vinegar
- 4 cloves garlic, minced
- 6 dried red chilies, seeded and crumbled

DIRECTIONS:

1. Put the garlic, chilies, green onions, and ginger in a food processor or blender and process to make a paste.
2. Heat the oil in a wok or frying pan, put in the paste, and stir-fry for four to five minutes. Turn off the heat and allow the mixture to cool completely.
3. In a small deep cooking pan, bring the vinegar to its boiling point. Put in the sugar and the lemongrass; decrease the heat and simmer for about twenty minutes.
4. Mix in the reserved paste.

YELLOW BEAN SAUCE

Yield: Approximately 1 cup

INGREDIENTS:

- 1 (½-inch) piece ginger, peeled and chopped
- 1 medium to big onion, minced
- 1 teaspoon ground coriander
- 2 serrano chilies, seeded and chopped
- 2 tablespoons lime juice
- 2 tablespoons vegetable oil
- 2 tablespoons water
- 4 tablespoons fermented yellow beans (fermented soy beans)

DIRECTIONS:

1. In a moderate-sized-sized sauté pan, heat the oil on moderate heat. Put in the onion and chilies, and sauté until the onion becomes translucent. Mix in the ginger and coriander, and carry on cooking for half a minute.
2. Put in the beans, lime juice, and water, and simmer using low heat for about ten minutes.
3. Move the mixture to a blender and process until the desired smoothness is achieved.

5-MINUTE DIPPING SAUCE

Yield: Approximately 4 tablespoons

INGREDIENTS:

- ½ teaspoon dried red pepper flakes
- 1 tablespoon fish sauce
- 1 tablespoon lime juice
- 1 teaspoon minced fresh ginger
- 1 teaspoon sugar

DIRECTIONS:

1. In a small container, dissolve the sugar in 1 tablespoon of water.
2. Mix in the rest of the ingredients; tweak seasonings if required. Serve at room temperature.

BANANA, TAMARIND, AND MINT SALSA

Yield: Approximately 2 cups

This unique salsa goes perfectly with roasted or grilled poultry or game.

INGREDIENTS:

- ¼ cup Tamarind Concentrate (Page 20)
- 1 roasted red jalapeño, seeded and chopped
- 1 tablespoon chopped fresh mint
- 1 tablespoon lime juice
- 1 teaspoon brown sugar
- 4 ripe bananas, peeled and finely diced

DIRECTIONS:

1. Lightly fold all the ingredients together.

GINGER-LEMONGRASS VINAIGRETTE

Yield: Approximately 1 quart

INGREDIENTS:

- ¼ cup grated fresh gingerroot
- 1 quart rice wine vinegar
- 2 stalks lemongrass, outer leaves removed and discarded, inner core slightly mashed

DIRECTIONS:

1. Mix all the ingredients in a nonreactive pot and simmer using low heat for half an hour.
2. Turn off the heat and allow it to stand overnight. Strain before you serve.

JALAPEÑO-LIME VINAIGRETTE

INGREDIENTS:

- 1 cup vegetable or canola oil
- 1 jalapeño, seeded and chopped
- 1 tablespoon sugar
- 1 cup lime juice
- Salt and pepper to taste

DIRECTIONS:

1. Put the jalapeño, lime juice, sugar, and salt and pepper in a food processor; blend for a minute.
2. While continuing to blend, slowly put in the oil; blend for half a minute or until well blended.

MANGO-CUCUMBER SALSA

Yield: Approximately 2 cups

INGREDIENTS:

- ¼ cup cut green onion
- ¼ cup orange juice
- 1 firm, ripe mango, peeled, seeded, and slice into ¼-inch dice
- 1 medium cucumber, seeded and slice into ¼-inch dice
- 1 teaspoon vegetable oil

- 2 teaspoons lime juice
- Salt and pepper to taste

DIRECTIONS:

1. Mix all the ingredients in a small container.

MANGO-PINEAPPLE SALSA

Yield: Approximately 4 cups

INGREDIENTS:

- ¼ cup snipped chives
- ½ cup diced red onion
- 1 cup diced pineapple
- 1 cup mango pieces
- 1 cup seeded and chopped tomato
- 1 serrano chili, seeded and chopped
- 2 tablespoons lime juice
- 2 tablespoons vegetable oil Salt and pepper to taste
- 3 tablespoons chopped cilantro

DIRECTIONS:

1. Mix all the ingredients in a small container.
2. Cover and place in your fridge for minimum 2 hours before you serve.

MINT-CILANTRO "CHUTNEY"

Yield: Approximately 2 cups

INGREDIENTS:

- ½ teaspoon minced honey
- ¾ cup packed cilantro
- ¾ cup packed mint leaves
- 2 teaspoons honey
- 3 tablespoons sour cream
- 1 cup unsalted peanuts, toasted
- Salt and pepper to taste

DIRECTIONS:

1. Put the peanuts in a food processor and finely grind.

2. Put in the rest of the ingredients to the processor and blend until well blended.

MINTY DIPPING SAUCE

Yield: Approximately 1 cup

INGREDIENTS:

- ¼ cup chopped mint leaves
- ¼ cup lime juice
- 1 serrano chili, seeded and diced
- 1 tablespoon grated lime zest
- 2 cloves garlic, minced
- 2 tablespoons fish sauce

DIRECTIONS:

1. Put all the ingredients in a blender and process until the desired smoothness is achieved.

2. Serve with a variety of grilled, skewered meats and raw or blanched vegetables.

LIME-GINGER FILLETS

Yield: Servings 2–4

INGREDIENTS:

- ½ teaspoon ground ginger
- ½ teaspoon salt
- 2 teaspoons lime zest
- 4 fish fillets, such as whitefish, perch, or pike
- 4 tablespoons unsalted butter, at room temperature
- Salt and freshly ground black pepper

DIRECTIONS:

1. Preheat your broiler.

2. In a small container, meticulously mix the butter, lime zest, ginger, and ½ teaspoon salt.

3. Lightly flavor the fillets with salt and pepper and place on a baking sheet.

4. Broil for about four minutes. Brush each fillet with some of the lime-ginger butter and continue to broil for a minute or until the fish is done to your preference.

MARINATED STEAMED FISH

Yield: Servings 4

INGREDIENTS:

- 1 big mushroom, thinly cut
- 1 tablespoon cut jalapeño pepper
- 1 tablespoon shrimp paste
- 1 tablespoon soy sauce
- 1 teaspoon Tabasco
- 1 whole lean flatfish (such as redfish, flounder, or bass), cleaned
- 2 green onions, finely cut
- 2 tablespoons grated ginger
- 3 tablespoons fish sauce
- Vegetable oil

DIRECTIONS:

1. Swiftly wash the fish under cold water. Pat dry using paper towels. Using a sharp knife, deeply score the fish three to 4 times on each side.
2. Mix together all of the rest of the ingredients except the vegetable oil.
3. Put the fish in a big plastic bag. Pour the marinade over the fish and seal. Allow the fish to marinate for approximately 1 hour in your fridge.
4. Fill the base of a tiered steamer full of water. Bring the water to its boiling point.
5. Meanwhile, lightly coat the rack with vegetable oil. Put the fish on the rack.
6. Put the rack over the boiling water, cover, and allow to steam for fifteen to twenty minutes, until the flesh of the fish appears opaque when pierced using a knife.

FRIED RICE WITH CHINESE OLIVES

Yield: Servings 2–3

INGREDIENTS:

- ½ cup ground pork or chicken
- 10 Chinese olives, pitted and chopped
- 3 cloves garlic, minced
- 3 cups day-old cooked rice Fish sauce (not necessary)
- 3 tablespoons vegetable oil

- Chopped cilantro
- Cucumber slices
- Hot sauce
- Lime wedges

DIRECTIONS:

1. Heat the oil in a wok or big frying pan on medium. Put in the garlic and stir-fry for a short period of time. Put in the pork and olives. Stir-fry until the pork is thoroughly cooked and any juices that have collected have cooked off.
2. Put in the rice, breaking up any clumps, and stir-fry until the rice is hot. Adjust the saltiness with a small amount of fish sauce if required.
3. Serve accompanied by cucumber slices, lime wedges, chopped cilantro, and hot sauce.

FRIED RICE WITH PINEAPPLE AND SHRIMP

Yield: Servings 2–4

INGREDIENTS:

- ½ teaspoon curry powder
- ½ teaspoon shrimp paste
- ½ teaspoon turmeric
- 1 cup finely chopped onion
- 1 ripe whole pineapple
- 2 garlic cloves, thoroughly minced 10 ounces peeled shrimp, deveined and slice into ½-inch pieces
- 2¼ cups day-old, cooked Jasmine or other long grained rice
- 4 tablespoons vegetable oil
- Salt to taste
- Sugar to taste

DIRECTIONS:

1. To prepare the pineapple, cut it in half along the length, leaving the leaves undamaged on 1 side. Scoop out the pineapple flesh of both halves, leaving a ½-inch edge on the half with the leaves. Reserve the hollowed-out half to use as a serving container. Dice the pineapple fruit and save for later.
2. Preheat your oven to 350 degrees.

3. In a wok or heavy sauté pan, heat the oil on medium. Put in the onion and garlic, and sauté until the onion is translucent. Using a slotted spoon, remove the onions and garlic from the wok and save for later.

4. Put in the shrimp and sauté roughly one minute; remove and save for later.

5. Put in the turmeric, curry powder, and shrimp paste to the wok; stir-fry for a short period of time. Put in the rice and stir-fry for two to three minutes. Put in the pineapple and carry on cooking. Put in the reserved shrimp, onions, and garlic. Season to taste with salt and sugar.

6. Mound the fried rice into the pineapple "serving container." Put the pineapple on a baking sheet and bake for roughly ten minutes. Serve instantly.

FRIED RICE WITH TOMATOES

INGREDIENTS:

- 1 clove garlic, minced
- 1 green onion, trimmed and cut
- 1 medium onion, slivered
- 1 teaspoon fish sauce
- 1 teaspoon ground white pepper
- 1 teaspoon sugar
- 1 tomato, cut into 8–10 wedges
- 1 whole boneless, skinless chicken breast, cut into bitesized pieces
- 2 eggs
- 2 teaspoons soy sauce
- 3 tablespoons vegetable oil
- 4 cups cooked rice

DIRECTIONS:

1. In a big frying pan or wok, heat the vegetable oil on moderate to high. Put in the chicken pieces and the garlic, and stir-fry one minute.

2. Put in the onion and continue to stir-fry for another minute.

3. Break in the eggs, stirring thoroughly.

4. Mix in all the rest of the ingredients; stir-fry for two more minutes.

5. Serve instantly.

GINGER RICE

Yield: Servings 4–6

INGREDIENTS:

- 1 (½-inch) piece of gingerroot, peeled and thinly cut
- 1 red chili pepper, seeded and minced
- 1 stalk lemongrass, cut into rings (soft inner portion only)
- 1½ cups long-grained rice
- 2 tablespoons vegetable oil
- 2¾ cups water
- 2—3 green onions, cut into rings
- Juice of ½ lime
- Pinch of brown sugar
- Pinch of salt

DIRECTIONS:

1. In a moderate-sized-sized pot, heat the oil on moderate heat. Put in the gingerroot, lemongrass, green onions, and chili pepper; sautée. for two to three minutes.
2. Put in the rice, brown sugar, salt, and lime juice, and continue to sautée. for another two minutes. Put in the water to the pot and bring to its boiling point.
3. Reduce the heat, cover with a tight-fitting lid, and simmer for fifteen to twenty minutes, until the liquid is absorbed.

LEMON RICE

Yield: Servings 2–4

INGREDIENTS:

- ¼ cup cashew nuts, soaked in cold water for five minutes
- ¼ teaspoon mustard seed
- ½ teaspoon turmeric
- 1 cup basmati rice, soaked in cold water for thirty minutes
- 1 cups water Pinch of salt
- 1 green chili pepper, seeded and minced
- 1 tablespoon vegetable oil
- 8 fresh curry leaves

* Juice of ½ lemon

DIRECTIONS:

1. In a moderate-sized-sized pan, bring the water to its boiling point. Put in the salt, rice, and turmeric; reduce heat, cover, and simmer for about ten minutes. (At the end of the ten minutes, the rice will have absorbed all of the liquid.) Turn off the heat and allow to cool.

2. In a wok, heat the oil and stir-fry the chili pepper. Put in the nuts, mustard seed, and curry leaves; carry on cooking for another half a minute. Mix in the lemon juice. Put in the cooled rice to the wok and toss until heated.

SHRIMP RICE

Yield: Servings 4–6

INGREDIENTS:

* 1 ¾cups long-grained rice
* 1 medium to big onion, finely chopped
* 1 quart water
* 1 stalk lemongrass, halved and crushed (inner white potion only)
* 1 tablespoon lime juice
* 2 cloves garlic, finely chopped
* 2 red chili peppers, seeded, veined, and thoroughly minced
* 4 tablespoons fish sauce
* 5 tablespoons dried shrimp, soaked in cold water for about ten minutes
* 5 tablespoons vegetable oil
* Salt to taste

DIRECTIONS:

1. Make a shrimp paste by combining the dried shrimp, chili peppers, onion, and garlic in a blender or food processor and processing until the desired smoothness is achieved.

2. In a moderate-sized-sized deep cooking pan, warm the oil on moderate heat. Put in the shrimp paste and cook for three to four minutes, stirring continuously.

3. Put in the fish sauce, lime juice, and salt to the paste and stir until well mixed; set aside.

4. Pour the rice into a big pot and put the lemongrass on top. Put in the water and bring to its boiling point; reduce heat, cover, and simmer for fifteen minutes.

5. Take away the lemongrass stalk and mix in the shrimp paste. Carry on cooking for five to ten minutes or until the rice is done.

SWEET-SPICED FRIED RICE

Yield: Approximately 4 cups

INGREDIENTS:

- ½ teaspoon mace
- 1 (1-inch) cinnamon stick
- 1 bay leaf
- 1 tablespoon brown sugar
- 1½ cups long-grained rice (such as Jasmine)
- 2¼ cups water
- 3 cloves
- 3 tablespoons vegetable oil ½ onion, cut into rings
- Salt

DIRECTIONS:

1. Soak the rice in cold water for about twenty minutes.
2. In the meantime, heat the oil in a moderate-sized pot on moderate heat. Put in the onions and sauté until golden, roughly ten to fifteen minutes.
3. Put in the spices and sauté for another two minutes. Drizzle the brown sugar over the onion mixture and caramelize for one to two minutes, stirring continuously. Put in the rice and sautée. for another three minutes, stirring continuously.
4. Put in the salt and the water to the pot and bring to its boiling point. Decrease the heat, cover, and simmer until the rice is soft, roughly ten to fifteen minutes.
5. Take away the cinnamon stick and cloves before you serve.

VEGETARIAN FRIED RICE

Yield: Servings 4–6

INGREDIENTS:

- ½ cup finely diced onion
- ½ cup vegetable stock
- ½ teaspoon brown sugar
- ½ teaspoon ground turmeric
- 1 tablespoon finely chopped fresh gingerroot

- 2 garlic cloves, finely chopped
- 2 medium carrots, peeled and julienned into 1-inch pieces
- 2 red chili peppers, seeded, veined, and thinly cut
- 2 stalks of celery, cut
- 2 tablespoons vegetarian "oyster" sauce
- 3 cups day-old long-grained rice
- 3 tablespoons soy sauce
- 3 tablespoons vegetable oil, divided
- 4 scallions, cut
- 7 ounces green beans, trimmed and slice into 1-inch pieces
- 9 ounces tomatoes, peeled, seeded, and diced
- Grated zest and juice of ½ of a lime
- Salt and freshly ground pepper to taste

DIRECTIONS:

1. In a wok or big sauté pan, heat 2 tablespoons of the vegetable oil on moderate to high heat. Put in the rice and stir-fry for two to three minutes. Take away the rice from the wok and save for later.
2. Put in the remaining tablespoon of oil to the wok. Put in the onion, garlic, and ginger; sauté for a minute.
3. Put in the chilies, scallions, green beans, carrots, and celery; stir-fry for about three minutes.
4. Put in the stock and bring to its boiling point; decrease the heat and simmer for five minutes.
5. Put in the tomatoes and simmer for another two minutes.
6. Put in the "oyster" and soy sauces and turmeric. Sprinkle salt and pepper to taste.
7. Mix in the lime zest, lime juice, brown sugar, and rice. Mix until blended.

BANANA COCONUT SOUP

INGREDIENTS:

- 1 cinnamon stick
- 1 tablespoon lemon juice
- 2 tablespoons minced gingerroot
- 4 cups banana slices, plus extra for decoration
- 4 cups canned coconut milk
- Salt to taste

DIRECTIONS:

1. In a big deep cooking pan, bring the coconut milk to its boiling point. Put in the banana, ginger, cinnamon stick, lemon juice, and a pinch of salt. Decrease the heat and simmer for ten to fifteen minutes or until the banana is very tender.

2. Take away the cinnamon stick and let cool slightly.

3. Using a handheld blender (or a blender or food processor), purée the soup until the desired smoothness is achieved.

4. Serve the soup in preheated bowls, decorated with banana slices and coconut.

BANANAS POACHED IN COCONUT MILK

Yield: Servings 2–3

INGREDIENTS:

- ¼ teaspoon salt
- 1 cup sugar
- 2–3 small, slightly green bananas
- 4 cups coconut milk

DIRECTIONS:

1. Peel the bananas and slice them in half along the length.

2. Pour the coconut milk into a pan big enough to hold the bananas laid flat in a single layer. Put in the sugar and salt and bring to its boiling point.

3. Reduce the heat, put in the bananas, and simmer until the bananas are just warmed through, approximately 3 to five minutes.

4. Serve the bananas warm on small plates decorated with fresh coconut and pineapple wedges.

CITRUS FOOL

Yield: Servings 4

INGREDIENTS:

- ½ cup heavy cream
- ½ cup orange, lime, or lemon juice
- 1 big egg, beaten
- 2 (3-inch-long, ½-inch wide) strips of citrus zest, minced
- 3 tablespoons sugar
- 3 tablespoons unsalted butter

DIRECTIONS:

1. Put the juice in a small deep cooking pan. Over moderate to high heat, reduce the liquid by half.

2. Take away the pan from the heat and mix in the sugar and butter. Mix in the egg until well blended.

3. Return the pan to the burner and cook on medium-low heat for three to five minutes or until bubbles barely start to form.

4. Take away the pan from the heat and mix in the citrus zest. Put the pan in a container of ice and stir the mixture until it is cold.

5. In another container, whip the cream until firm. Fold the citrus mixture meticulously into the cream.

COCONUT CUSTARD

Yield: Servings 6

INGREDIENTS:

*   1 (16-ounce) can coconut cream
*   3 tablespoons butter
*   6 big eggs, lightly beaten
*   1 cup fine granulated sugar
*   Fresh tropical fruit (not necessary)

DIRECTIONS:

1. In a large, heavy-bottomed deep cooking pan, mix together the coconut cream and the sugar.

2. Over moderate heat, cook and stir the mixture until the sugar is thoroughly blended.

3. Lower the heat to low and mix in the eggs. Cook while stirring once in a while, until the mixture is thick and coats the back of a spoon, approximately ten to twelve minutes.

4. Take away the pan from the heat and put in the butter. Stir until the butter is completely melted and blended.

5. Pour the custard into six 4-ounce custard cups. Put the cups in a baking pan. Pour boiling water into the baking pan until it comes midway up the sides of the custard cups.

6. Cautiously move the baking pan to a preheated 325-degree oven. Bake the custards for thirty to forty minutes until set. (The tip of a knife should come out clean when inserted into the middle of the custard.)

7. Serve warm or at room temperature. Decorate using chopped tropical fruit, if you wish.

COCONUT-PINEAPPLE SOUFFLÉ FOR 2

Yield: 2

INGREDIENTS:

* ½ cup (½-inch) cubes ladyfingers or sponge cake
* 1 egg yolk
* 2 egg whites
* 2 tablespoons dark rum
* 2 tablespoons finely chopped fresh pineapple
* 2 tablespoons sugar
* 2½ tablespoons grated sweetened coconut
* Lemon juice
* Softened butter for the molds
* Sugar for the molds

DIRECTIONS:

1. Preheat your oven to 400 degrees.
2. Butter 2-¾ or 1-cup soufflée molds and then drizzle them with sugar. Place in your fridge the molds until ready to use.
3. Put the ladyfinger cubes in a small container. Pour the rum over the cubes and allow to soak for five minutes.
4. Squeeze the juice from the pineapple, saving both the pulp and 1 tablespoon of the juice.
5. In a small container, beat the egg yolk with the pineapple juice until very thick. Fold in the cake cubes, pineapple pulp, and coconut.
6. In another small container, beat the egg whites with a few drops of lemon juice until foamy. Slowly put in the 2 tablespoons of sugar, while continuing to beat until the whites are stiff and shiny.
7. Lightly fold the pineapple mixture into the egg whites.
8. Ladle the batter into the prepared molds and bake for eight to ten minutes or until puffy and mildly browned.

CRISPY CREPES WITH FRESH FRUIT

INGREDIENTS:

* ¼ cup shredded, unsweetened coconut
* 1 cup heavy cream
* 1 package frozen puff pastry sheets, thawed in accordance with package instructions
* 1 tablespoon unflavored rum or coconut-flavored rum
* 2 cups raspberries, blueberries, or other fresh fruit, the best 12 berries reserved for decoration

- 2 tablespoons confectioner's sugar, divided

DIRECTIONS:

1. Preheat your oven to 400 degrees.
2. Put the puff pastry sheet on a work surface and slice into 12 equalsized pieces. Put the pastry pieces on a baking sheet.
3. Bake the pastry roughly ten minutes. Take out of the oven and use a sifter to shake a small amount of the confectioner?s sugar over the puff pastry. Return to the oven and carry on baking for roughly five minutes or until golden. Put the puff pastry on a wire rack and let cool completely.
4. Put the berries in a food processor and for a short period of time process to make a rough purée.
5. Whip the cream with the rest of the confectioner's sugar until thick, but not firm. Mix in the coconut and the rum.
6. To serve, place 1 piece of puff pastry in the center of each serving plate, spoon some cream over the pastry, and then top with some purée. Put another pastry on top, decorate with some of the rest of the berries, any remaining juice from the purée, and a drizzle of confectioner's sugar.

FRESH ORANGES IN ROSE WATER

Yield: Servings 6–8

INGREDIENTS:

- 1½ cups sugar
- 3 cups water
- 4–6 teaspoons rose water
- 8 oranges

DIRECTIONS:

1. Peel and segment the oranges. Put them in a container, cover, and set aside in your fridge.
2. In a deep cooking pan, bring the water and the sugar to its boiling point over moderatehigh heat. Boil gently for fifteen to 20 or until the mixture becomes syrupy. Turn off the heat and mix in the rose water. Allow to cool to room temperature and then place in your fridge
3. To serve, place orange segments in individual dessert cups. Pour rose water syrup over the top.

LEMONGRASS CUSTARD

INGREDIENTS:

- ½ cup suga
- 2 cups whole milk

- 2 stalks fresh lemongrass, finely chopped (soft inner portion only)
- 6 egg yolks

DIRECTIONS:

1. Preheat your oven to 275 degrees.
2. In a moderate-sized-sized deep cooking pan, on moderate to high heat, bring the milk and the lemongrass to its boiling point. Lower the heat and simmer for five minutes. Cover the milk mixture, remove the heat, and allow it to sit for about ten minutes on the burner.
3. In a mixing container, beat the egg yolks with the sugar until thick.
4. Strain the milk mixture through a fine-mesh sieve, then slowly pour it into the egg yolks, whisking continuously.
5. Split the mixture between 6 small custard cups and put the cups in a high-sided baking or roasting pan. Put in warm water to the pan so that it reaches to roughly an inch below the top of the custard cups. Cover the pan firmly using foil.
6. Put the pan in your oven and bake for roughly twenty minutes or until the custards are set on the sides but still slightly wobbly in the middle.

MANGO FOOL

Yield: Servings 4–6

INGREDIENTS:

- ¼ cup sugar
- 1 cup heavy cream
- 1 tablespoon confectioners' sugar
- 2 ripe mangoes, peeled and flesh cut from the pits 2 tablespoons lime juice
- Crystallized ginger (not necessary)
- Mint leaves (not necessary)

DIRECTIONS:

1. Put the mangoes in a food processor with the lime juice and sugar. Puréee until the desired smoothness is achieved.
2. In a big container beat the heavy cream with the confectioners' sugar until firm.
3. Thoroughly fold the mango purée into the heavy cream.
4. Serve in goblets decorated with crystallized ginger or sprigs of mint, if you wish.

MANGO SAUCE OVER ICE CREAM

Yield: 2 cups

INGREDIENTS:

- 1 banana, peeled and chopped
- 1 tablespoon brandy (not necessary)
- 2 mangoes, peeled, pitted, and diced
- 1 cup (or to taste) sugar
- Juice of 2 big limes (or to taste)
- Vanilla ice cream

DIRECTIONS:

1. In a moderate-sized-sized deep cooking pan using low heat, simmer the mangoes, banana, sugar, and lime juice for thirty minutes, stirring regularly.
2. Put in the brandy and simmer 5 more minutes.
3. Turn off the heat and let cool slightly or to room temperature.
4. To serve, scoop ice cream into individual serving bowls. Ladle sauce over top.

PINEAPPLE RICE

Yield: Servings 4–6

INGREDIENTS:

- ¼ cup sugar
- ½ cup short-grained rice
- 1 ripe pineapple
- 2 teaspoons chopped crystallized ginger, divided
- 3 tablespoons roasted cashew nuts, chopped
- Pinch of salt
- Zest and juice of 1 lemon

DIRECTIONS:

1. Chop the pineapple in half along the length, leaving the leaves undamaged on 1 side. Scoop out the pineapple flesh of both halves, leaving a ½-inch edge on the half with the leaves. Dice the pineapple fruit from 1 half and purée the fruit from the other half in a food processor together with the sugar and salt; set aside.
2. Strain the fruit purée through a fine-mesh sieve into a measuring cup. Put in enough water to make 1¾ cups. Move to a small deep cooking pan and bring to its boiling point on moderate to high heat.

3. Wash and drain the rice. Mix the rice into the pineapple purée. Mix in the lemon zest, lemon juice, and 1 teaspoon of the ginger. Bring to its boiling point; reduce heat, cover, and simmer until the liquid has been absorbed, approximately twenty minutes.

4. Combine the reserved pineapple cubes into the rice.

5. To serve, spoon the rice into the hollowed out pineapple that has the leaves. Decorate using the rest of the ginger and the roasted cashews.

PINEAPPLE-MANGO SHERBET

Yield: Servings 4–6

INGREDIENTS:

- ½ cup plain yogurt
- 1 big orange, peeled and segmented
- 1 cup pineapple pieces
- 1 tablespoon lime zest
- 1 teaspoon orange-flavored liqueur (not necessary)
- 2 mangoes, peeled, pitted, and slice into 1-inch cubes
- 1 cup sugar

DIRECTIONS:

1. Put the orange segments, mango cubes, and pineapple pieces on a baking sheet lined with waxed paper; store in your freezer for 30 to forty-five minutes or until just frozen.

2. Move the fruit to a food processor. Put in the lime zest and sugar, and pulse until well blended.

3. While the machine runs, add the yogurt and liqueur. Process for another three minutes or until the mixture is fluffy.

4. Pour the mixture into an 8″ × 8″ pan, cover using foil, and freeze overnight.

5. To serve, let the sherbet temper at room temperature for ten to fifteen minutes, then scoop into glass dishes.

PUMPKIN CUSTARD

Yield: Servings 4

INGREDIENTS:

- 1 small cooking pumpkin
- 5 eggs
- 1 cup brown sugar

DIRECTIONS:

1. With a small sharp knife, cautiously chop the top off of the pumpkin.
2. Using a spoon, remove and discard the seeds and most of the tender flesh; set the pumpkin aside.
3. In a moderate-sized-sized mixing container, whisk the eggs together. Mix in the brown sugar, salt, and coconut cream until well blended.
4. Pour the mixture into the pumpkin.
5. Put the pumpkin in a steamer and allow to steam for roughly twenty minutes or until the custard is set.

PUMPKIN SIMMERED IN COCONUT MILK

Yield: Servings 4

INGREDIENTS:

- ½ cup coconut milk
- ½ teaspoon salt
- 1 cup water
- 2 cups fresh pumpkin meat cut into big julienned pieces (acorn squash is a good substitute)
- 1 cup brown sugar

DIRECTIONS:

1. Place the water and the coconut milk in a moderate-sized pan using low heat. Put in the salt and half of the sugar; stir until well blended. Adjust the sweetness to your preference by put in more water or sugar if required.
2. Put in the julienned pumpkin to the pan and bring to its boiling point on moderate heat. Reduce to a simmer and cook until soft, approximately 5 to ten minutes depending on both the texture of the pumpkin and your own preference.
3. The pumpkin may be served hot, warm, or cold.

STEAMED COCONUT CAKES

Yield: 10 cakes

INGREDIENTS:

- ¼ cup all-purpose flour
- ½ cup coconut milk
- ½ cup grated sweet coconut
- ½ cup rice flour
- 4 tablespoons finely granulated sugar

- 5 eggs
- Pinch of salt

DIRECTIONS:

1. In a big mixing container, beat the eggs and the sugar together until thick and pale in color.
2. Put in the rice flours and salt.
3. Beating continuously, slowly pour in the coconut milk. Beat the batter for 3 more minutes.
4. Bring some water to boil in a steamer big enough to hold 10 small ramekins. When the water starts to boil, put the ramekins in the steamer to heat for a couple of minutes.
5. Split the shredded coconut uniformly between all of the ramekins and use a spoon to compact it on the bottom of the cups.
6. Pour the batter uniformly between the cups. Steam for about ten minutes.
7. Take away the cakes from the cups the moment they are sufficiently cool to handle.
8. Serve warm or at room temperature.

STICKY RICE WITH COCONUT CREAM SAUCE

Yield: Servings 6

INGREDIENTS:

- 1 cup coconut cream
- 1 teaspoon salt
- 3 cups cooked Sweet Sticky Rice
- 4 ripe mangoes, thinly cut (or other tropical fruits)
- 4 tablespoons sugar

DIRECTIONS:

1. For the sauce, put the coconut cream, sugar, and salt in a small deep cooking pan. Stir to blend and bring to its boiling point on moderate to high heat. Decrease the heat and simmer for five minutes.
2. To serve, position mango slices on each plate. Put a mound of rice next to the fruit. Top the rice with some of the sauce.

SWEET STICKY RICE

Yield: Servings 6

INGREDIENTS:

* ½ cup granulated sugar
* ½ teaspoon salt
* 1 cups canned coconut milk
* 1½ cups white glutinous rice

DIRECTIONS:

1. Put the rice in a container and put in enough water to completely cover the rice. Soak for minimum 4 hours or overnight. Drain.
2. Coat a steamer basket with wet cheesecloth. Spread the rice uniformly over the cheesecloth. Put the container over quickly boiling water. Cover and steam until soft, approximately twenty-five minutes; set aside.
3. In a moderate-sized-sized deep cooking pan, mix the coconut milk, sugar, and salt and heat on moderate to high. Stir until the sugar is thoroughly blended. Pour over the rice, stir until blended, and allow to rest for half an hour
4. To serve, place in small bowls or on plates. Decorate using mangoes, papayas, or other tropical fruit.

TARO BALLS POACHED IN COCONUT MILK

INGREDIENTS:

* 1 cup brown sugar
* 1 cup cooked taro, mashed
* 1 cup corn flour
* 2 cups glutinous rice flour
* 4 cups coconut milk
* Fresh tropical fruit (not necessary)
* teaspoon salt

DIRECTIONS:

1. In a big mixing container, mix the rice and the flours.
2. Put in the mashed taro and knead to make a tender dough.
3. Roll into little bite-sized balls and save for later.
4. In a moderate-sized to big deep cooking pan, heat the coconut milk using low heat.
5. Put in the brown sugar and the salt, stirring until blended.

6. Bring the mixture to a low boil and put in the taro balls.

7. Poach the balls for five to ten minutes or until done to your preference.

8. Serve hot in small glass bowls, decorated with tropical fruit.

TOFU WITH SWEET GINGER

Yield: 3 cups of sauce

INGREDIENTS:

- 1 (2- to 3-inch) piece of ginger, peeled and smashed using the back of a knife
- 1 12-ounce package tender tofu
- 3 cups water
- 1 cup brown sugar

DIRECTIONS:

1. Put the water, ginger, and brown sugar in a small deep cooking pan. Bring to its boiling point using high heat. Lower the heat to a simmer and allow the sauce to cook for minimum ten minutes. (The longer you allow the mixture to cook, the spicier it will get.)

2. To serve, spoon some of the tofu into dessert bowls and pour some sauce over the top. (This sauce is equally good over plain yogurt.)

TROPICAL COCONUT RICE

Yield: Servings 6–8

INGREDIENTS:

- ¼ cup toasted coconut
- 1 cup coconut cream
- 2 cups short-grained rice
- 2 cups water

DIRECTIONS:

1. Place the rice, water, and coconut cream in a moderate-sized deep cooking pan and mix thoroughly. Bring to its boiling point on moderate to high heat. Decrease the heat and cover with a tight-fitting lid. Cook for fifteen to twenty minutes or until all of the liquid has been absorbed.

2. Allow the rice rest off the heat for five minutes.

3. Fluff the rice and mix in the toasted coconut and fruit.

TROPICAL FRUIT WITH GINGER CREÈME ANGLAISE

Yield: 1½ cups

INGREDIENTS:

- (1-inch) pieces peeled gingerroot, slightly mashed
- 1 cup half-and-half
- 2 tablespoons sugar A variety of tropical fruits, cut
- 3 egg yolks

DIRECTIONS:

1. In a small heavy deep cooking pan on moderate to low heat, bring the ginger and the half-and-half to a slight simmer. Do not boil.
2. Meanwhile, whisk together the eggs yolks and the sugar.
3. Slowly pour the hot half-and-half into the egg mixture, stirring continuously so that the eggs do not cook.
4. Pour the custard back into the deep cooking pan and cook on moderate to low heat, stirring continuously using a wooden spoon for five minutes or until slightly thickened.
5. Pour the crèmes anglaise through a mesh strainer into a clean container and let cool completely.
6. Pour over slices of your favorite tropical fruits.

WATERMELON ICE

Yield: Servings 6–8

INGREDIENTS:

- ½ cup sugar
- 1 (3-pound) piece of watermelon, rind cut away, seeded, and cut into little chunks (reserve a small amount for decoration if you wish)
- 1 cup water
- 1 tablespoon lime juice
- Mint sprigs (not necessary)

DIRECTIONS:

1. Put the water and sugar in a small deep cooking pan and bring to its boiling point. Turn off the heat and let cool to room temperature, stirring regularly. Set the pan in a container of ice and continue to stir the syrup until cold.
2. Put the watermelon, syrup, and lime juice in a blender and purée until the desired smoothness is achieved.
3. Pour the purée through a sieve into a 9-inch baking pan. Cover the pan using foil.
4. Put into your freezer the purée for eight hours or until frozen.
5. To serve, scrape the frozen purée with the tines of a fork. Ladle the scrapings into pretty glass goblets and decorate with a small piece of watermelon or mint sprigs.

FRESH COCONUT JUICE

Yield: Servings 1–2 depending on the size of the coconut.

INGREDIENTS:

- 1 young coconut
- Ice
- Sprig of mint for decoration

DIRECTIONS:

1. Using a meat cleaver, make a V-shaped slice on the top of the coconut.
2. Pour the juice over a glass of ice.
3. Decorate using a mint sprig.

GINGER TEA

Yield: 8 cups

INGREDIENTS:

- ½-¾ cup sugar
- 1 big branch (roughly
- 8 cups water
- pound) of ginger, cut into long pieces

DIRECTIONS:

1. Bring the water to its boiling point in a big pan. Put in the ginger, reduce heat, and simmer for ten to twenty minutes, depending on how strong you prefer your tea.
2. Take away the ginger and put in the sugar to taste, stirring until it is thoroughly blended.
3. Serve hot or over ice.

ICED SWEET TEA

Yield: slightly more than 1 cup.

INGREDIENTS:

- 1 cup hot water
- 1 tablespoon sugar
- 1 tablespoon sweetened condensed milk
- 1 teaspoon milk
- 1–2 tablespoons Thai tea leaves
- Ice

DIRECTIONS:

1. Place the sugar and sweetened condensed milk into a big glass.
2. Put the tea leaves into a tea ball and place it in the glass.
3. Put in the hot water. Allow to steep until done to your preferred strength.
4. Stir to dissolve the sugar and sweetened condensed milk.
5. Put in ice and top with milk.

LEMONGRASS TEA

Yield: 8 cups

INGREDIENTS:

- ¼– cup sugar
- 1 cup lemongrass stalks, chopped
- 8 cups water

DIRECTIONS:

1. Bring the water to its boiling point in a big pan. Put in the lemongrass, turn off the heat, and allow to steep for ten to twenty minutes, depending on how strong you prefer your tea.
2. Take away the lemongrass and put in the sugar to taste, stirring until it is thoroughly blended.
3. Serve hot or over ice.

MANGO BELLINI

Yield: 1 glass

INGREDIENTS:

- ½ teaspoon lemon juice

- 1 teaspoon mango schnapps

- 2 tablespoons puréed mango

- Chilled champagne

DIRECTIONS:

1. Put the mango purée, mango schnapps, and lemon juice in a champagne flute.
2. Fill the flute with champagne and stir.

ROYAL THAI KIR

Yield: 1 glass

INGREDIENTS:

- 1–2 teaspoons creème de mango or mango schnapps

- Chilled dry champagne

DIRECTIONS:

1. Pour the creème into a champagne flute and fill with champagne.

SUPER-SIMPLE THAI ICED TEA

Yield: Approximately 1 cup

INGREDIENTS:

- 2 tablespoons sugar

- 1 cup hot water

- Ice

- 1–2 tablespoons Thai tea leaves

DIRECTIONS:

1. Place the sugar into a big glass.
2. Put the tea leaves in a tea ball and place it in the glass.
3. Put in the hot water. Allow to steep until done to your preferred strength.
4. Stir to dissolve the sugar and put in ice.

THAI "MARTINIS"

Yield: 3 quarts

INGREDIENTS:

- 1 bottle coconut rum
- 1 bottle dark rum
- 1 bottle light rum
- 1 whole ripe pineapple
- 3 stalks lemongrass, trimmed, cut into 3-inch lengths and tied in a bundle

DIRECTIONS:

1. Take away the pineapple greens and then quarter the rest of the fruit. Put the pineapple quarters and the lemongrass bundle in a container big enough to hold all of the liquor.
2. Pour the rums over the fruit and stir until blended. Cover the container and let infuse for minimum one week at room temperature.
3. Take away the lemongrass bundle and discard.
4. Take away the pineapple quarters and slice into slices for decoration.
5. To serve, pour some of the rum into a martini shaker filled with ice; shake thoroughly. Pour into martini glasses and decorate with a pineapple slice.

THAI ICED TEA

Yield: Approximately 8 cups

INGREDIENTS:

- 1 cup sugar
- 1 cup Thai tea leaves
- 1–1½ cups half-and-half
- 6 cups water
- Ice

DIRECTIONS:

1. Bring the water to boil in a moderate-sized pot. Turn off the heat and put in the tea leaves, pushing them into the water until they are completely submerged. Steep roughly five minutes or until the liquid is a bright orange.
2. Strain through a fine-mesh sieve or coffee strainer.
3. Mix in the sugar until thoroughly blended.
4. Allow the tea to reach room temperature and then place in your fridge
5. To serve, pour the tea over ice cubes, leaving room at the top of the glass to pour in three to 4 tablespoons of half-and-half; stir for a short period of time to blend.

THAI LIMEADE

Yield: 9 cups

INGREDIENTS:

- 1–½ cup sugar
- 1 cup lime juice, lime rinds reserved
- 8 cups water
- Salt to taste (not necessary)

DIRECTIONS:

1. Mix the lime juice and the sugar; set aside.
2. Bring the water to boil in a big pot. Put in the lime rinds and turn off the heat. Allow to steep for ten to fifteen minutes. Take away the lime rinds.
3. Put in the lime juice mixture to the hot water, stirring to completely dissolve the sugar. Put in salt if you wish.
4. Serve over ice.

THAI-INSPIRED SINGAPORE SLING

Yield: 1 cocktail

INGREDIENTS:

- ¼– cup pineapple juice Mint sprig (not necessary)
- 1 tablespoon cherry brandy
- 1 tablespoon lime juice
- 1 tablespoon orange liqueur
- 1 teaspoon brown sugar
- 2 tablespoons whiskey
- Dash of bitters

DIRECTIONS:

1. Put all of the ingredients into a cocktail shaker and shake thoroughly to blend.
2. Serve over crushed ice and decorate with a sprig of mint if you wish.

TROPICAL FRUIT COCKTAIL

Yield: 3–4 cups

INGREDIENTS:

- 1 small mango, papaya, banana, or other tropical fruit, peeled and roughly chopped (reserve a small amount for decoration if you wish)
- 1 tablespoon brown sugar
- 1 teaspoon grated ginger
- 1/ cups orange or grapefruit juice
- 1/ cups pineapple juice
- 1–½ cup (or to taste) rum
- 4 tablespoons lime or lemon juice

DIRECTIONS:

1. Put the chopped fruit, lime juice, ginger, and sugar in a blender and process until the desired smoothness is achieved.
2. Put in the rest of the ingredients to the blender and pulse until well blended.
3. To serve, pour over crushed ice and garnish with fruit slices of your choice.

ASIAN 3-BEAN SALAD

Yield: Servings 4–6

INGREDIENTS:

- ½ teaspoon lime zest
- 1 (14-ounce) can black beans
- 1 (14-ounce) can garbanzo beans
- 1 (14-ounce) can red kidney beans
- 1 cup chopped cilantro
- 1 moderate-sized red onion, chopped
- 1 teaspoon minced jalapeño
- 3 cloves garlic, minced
- 3 tablespoons rice vinegar
- 4 tablespoons olive oil
- Salt and pepper to taste

DIRECTIONS:

1. Put all the beans in a colander. Thoroughly wash under cool running water. Drain and save for later.
2. Mix together all the rest of the ingredients and pour over beans; stir until blended.

3. Place in your fridge overnight, stirring once in a while. Sprinkle with salt and pepper.

ASIAN CARROT STICKS

Yield: Servings 4–6

INGREDIENTS:

- –¼ teaspoon cayenne pepper
- ½–½ teaspoons paprika
- ½–1 teaspoon Chinese 5-spice powder
- 1 pound thin carrots, peeled and slice into quarters along the length
- 2 cloves garlic, minced
- 2 tablespoons rice vinegar
- 3 tablespoons chopped cilantro
- 4 tablespoons olive oil
- 4 tablespoons water
- Salt and pepper to taste

DIRECTIONS:

1. Put the carrots in a pan big enough to hold them easily.
2. Cover the carrots with water and bring to its boiling point using high heat. Drain the carrots and return them to the pan.
3. Put in the 4 tablespoons of water, the olive oil, and the garlic; bring to its boiling point, reduce to a simmer, and cook until just soft. Drain.
4. In a small container, mix together rest of the ingredients; pour over the carrots, tossing to coat.
5. Sprinkle salt and pepper to taste.
6. The carrots may be eaten instantly, but develop a richer flavor if allowed to marinate for a few hours.

ASIAN COUSCOUS SALAD

Yield: Servings 8–10

INGREDIENTS:

- ½ cup vegetable oil
- 1 clove garlic, minced
- 1 moderate-sized red onion, chopped
- 1 packed cup basil
- 1 packed cup cilantro

- 1 packed cup mint
- 1 pound snow peas, trimmed
- 1 red bell pepper, cored, seeded, and chopped
- 1 yellow bell pepper, cored, seeded, and chopped
- 1–2 jalapeño chilies, seeded and finely chopped
- 2 tablespoons lemon juice
- 2¾ cups couscous
- 3 tablespoons lime juice
- 3½ cups boiling water, divided
- 5–7 green onions, trimmed and thinly cut
- Salt and freshly ground black pepper to taste

DIRECTIONS:

1. Put the snow peas, peppers, onions, chilies, garlic, and couscous in a big container; toss to blend.
2. Pour 3 cups of the boiling water over the couscous mixture, cover firmly, and allow it to stand at room temperature for an hour.
3. Put in the remaining fi cup boiling water and all the rest of the ingredients to the couscous; toss together, cover, and allow it to stand for minimum 30 more minutes.
4. Sprinkle with salt and freshly ground black pepper.

ASIAN MARINARA SAUCE

Yield: Approximately 2 cups

INGREDIENTS:

- 1 (1-inch) piece of ginger, peeled and minced
- 1 cup water
- 1 medium onion, chopped
- 1 pound chopped canned tomatoes with the juice
- 1 teaspoon salt
- 1 teaspoon sugar
- 1—3 serrano chilies, seeded and minced
- 2 tablespoons vegetable oil

DIRECTIONS:

1. In a big deep cooking pan, heat the oil on moderate heat.

2. Put in the onion and ginger and sauté for a couple of minutes.

3. Put in the chilies and carry on cooking one minute more.

4. Mix in the water, tomatoes, salt, and sugar. Decrease the heat to low and simmer for minimum 30 minutes.

ASIAN RATATOUILLE

Yield: Servings 6–8

INGREDIENTS:

- ½ teaspoon salt
- ½-inch cubes
- ¾ cup vegetable stock
- 1 cup cut mushrooms
- 1 onion, slivered
- 1 red bell pepper, cored, seeded, and julienned
- 1 tablespoon chopped cilantro
- 1 tablespoon cornstarch
- 1 tablespoon dry sherry
- 1 teaspoon minced garlic
- 1 teaspoon minced ginger
- 2 Japanese eggplants (approximately 1 pound), cut into
- 2 ribs of celery, cut
- 2 small zucchini, halved along the length and cut
- 2 tablespoons soy sauce
- 2 teaspoons Plum Dipping Sauce (Page 34)
- 3 tablespoons sesame oil
- 3 tablespoons vegetable oil

DIRECTIONS:

1. Put the eggplant in a colander and drizzle with the salt. Allow to rest for half an hour

2. In a big ovenproof pot, heat the sesame oil on medium. Put in the celery, onion, and red bell pepper; sautée for five minutes. Take the vegetables out of the pan and save for later.

3. Put in the vegetable oil to the pot. Sauté the zucchini, mushrooms, and eggplant for five minutes. Mix in the celery, onion, and bell pepper and save for later.

4. In a small mixing container, whisk together the stock, soy sauce, sherry, and cornstarch. Pour over the vegetables and stir until blended.
5. Bake, covered, in a 350-degree oven for forty minutes.
6. Mix in the garlic, ginger, and plum sauce. Cover and carry on baking for another ten minutes.

ASIAN-INSPIRED CHICKEN AND WILD RICE SOUP

Yield: Servings 6–8

INGREDIENTS:

- 1 tablespoon vegetable oil
- 1–2 garlic cloves, minced
- 2 tablespoons fish sauce
- 2 whole boneless, skinless chicken breasts, trimmed and slice into fine strips
- 2–3 teaspoons minced ginger
- 6 cups low-fat, low-salt chicken broth

DIRECTIONS:

1. In a big soup pot, heat the oil on moderate to high. Put in the chicken strips and sauté for two to three minutes.
2. Put in the garlic and gingerroot and sauté for one more minute.
3. Mix in the fish sauce, broth, and rice. Bring to its boiling point; reduce heat, cover, and simmer for about ten minutes.
4. Put in the green onions and snow peas; simmer to heat through.
5. Adjust seasoning with salt and freshly ground white pepper to taste.

CHICKEN SALAD — 1

Yield: Servings 4

INGREDIENTS:

For the dressing:

- ¼ cup vegetable oil
- ½; teaspoon (or to taste) salt
- 1 tablespoon soy sauce

- 2 tablespoons rice wine vinegar
- 2 teaspoons grated gingerroot
- Pinch of sugar

For the salad:

- 1 cup bean sprouts
- 1 medium head of Chinese cabbage, shredded
- 1 tablespoon toasted sesame seeds
- 2 cups chopped cooked chicken
- 3 green onions, trimmed and cut
- 4 ounces snow peas, trimmed

DIRECTIONS:

1. Put the salad dressing ingredients in a small container and whisk vigorously to blend.
2. In a moderate-sized-sized container, mix the chicken, snow peas, green onions, and bean sprouts. Put in the dressing and toss to coat.
3. To serve, position the cabbage on a serving platter. Mound the chicken salad over the cabbage. Decorate using the sesame seeds.

CHICKEN SALAD — 2

Yield: Servings 4–6

INGREDIENTS:

- ¼ cup chopped cilantro, plus extra for decoration
- ¼ pound rice sticks
- 1 cup cut scallions
- 1 tablespoon dry sherry
- 1 tablespoon soy sauce
- 1 tablespoon vegetable oil
- 1 teaspoon sesame oil
- 2 whole boneless, skinless chicken breasts
- 3 tablespoons hoisin sauce, divided
- 3 tablespoons peanuts, chopped
- 3 tablespoons sesame seeds, toasted
- 4 tablespoons lime juice

- Bibb or romaine lettuce leaves
- Peanut oil for frying

DIRECTIONS:

1. Mix 1 tablespoon of the hoisin sauce, the soy sauce, and the sherry in a moderate-sized container. Put in the chicken breasts and marinate for twenty minutes to half an hour.
2. Heat the vegetable oil in a big frying pan on moderate to high heat. Put in the chicken breasts, saving for later the marinade. Brown the breasts on both sides. Put in the reserved marinade to the frying pan, cover, and cook on moderate to low heat until soft, approximately twenty minutes.
3. Allow the chicken to cool completely, then shred it into bite-sized pieces; set aside.
4. In a moderate-sized-sized container, mix the shredded chicken with the rest of the hoisin sauce, the lime juice, sesame oil, sesame seeds, peanuts, scallions, and cilantro. Put in the shredded chicken and stir to coat.
5. Put in roughly an inch of peanut oil to a big frying pan and heat on high until the oil is super hot, but not smoking.
6. Put in the rice sticks cautiously and fry for roughly 6 to 8 seconds or until puffed and golden; turn the rice sticks using tongs and fry for another 6 to 8 seconds. Take away the rice sticks to a stack of paper towels to drain.
7. Toss about of the rice sticks with the chicken mixture.
8. To serve, place a mound of salad on a lettuce leaf on the center of each plate. Top with the rest of the rice sticks and decorate with additional cilantro.

CHICKEN SALAD—3

Yield: 3–4 cups

INGREDIENTS:

- ½ cup soy sauce
- ½ cup super slimly cut celery
- ½ teaspoon sesame oil (not necessary)
- 1 (¼-inch) piece ginger, peeled and minced
- 1 clove garlic, minced
- 1 cup cooked chicken meat
- 1 scallion, thinly cut
- 1 tablespoon sugar
- 1 teaspoon vegetable oil

- 2 tablespoons rice vinegar
- cups shredded bok choy

DIRECTIONS:

1. In a moderate-sized-sized container, toss together the chicken, bok choy, celery, and scallion.
2. In a small container, meticulously whisk together the rest of the ingredients. Pour over the salad and toss thoroughly to blend.

CRAZY COCONUT PIE

Yield: 1 (10-inch) pie

INGREDIENTS:

- ½ cup flour
- ¾ cup sugar
- ¾ stick of butter, melted
- 1 cup sweetened shredded coconut
- 1½ teaspoons vanilla
- 2 cups milk
- 4 eggs

DIRECTIONS:

1. Preheat your oven to 350 degrees. Grease and flour a 10-inch pie plate.
2. Put all of the ingredients in a blender and blend for a minute. Pour the batter into the readied pan.
3. Bake for about forty-five minutes or until golden on top.

CREAM OF COCONUT CRABMEAT DIP

Yield: Approximately 2 cups

INGREDIENTS:

- ¼ teaspoon salt 2 green onions, trimmed and thinly cut
- ¾ cup cream of coconut
- 1 jalapeño, seeded and minced
- 1 tablespoon lemon or lime juice
- 1¼ pounds (10 ounces) crabmeat, picked over to remove shell pieces
- 2 tablespoons chopped cilantro

- Ground white pepper to taste

DIRECTIONS:

1. In a small deep cooking pan, mix the cream of coconut, crabmeat, and salt; bring to a simmer on moderate to low heat. Simmer for five minutes.
2. Mix in the green onions, cilantro, lemon juice, jalapeño, and pepper. Pour into a serving dish and allow it to stand at room temperature until cool.
3. Serve with fresh vegetables and crackers.

CRUNCHY SPROUT SALAD

Yield: Servings 4

INGREDIENTS:

- ¼ cup rice vinegar
- 1 tablespoon sugar
- 2 cups sprouts of your choice
- 2 tablespoons fish or soy sauce
- 2 tablespoons vegetable oil
- 2 teaspoons grated gingerroot
- 6 cups baby greens (if possible an Asian mix)

DIRECTIONS:

1. In a big container whisk together the vinegar, fish sauce, vegetable oil, sugar, and gingerroot.
2. Put in the sprouts, toss to coat, and let marinate for half an hour
3. Put in the greens and toss until well blended.

GRILLED LOBSTER TAILS WITH A LEMONGRASS SMOKE

Yield: Servings 6

INGREDIENTS:

- 3–4 whole lemongrass stalks, bruised
- 6 (4–6 ounce) lobster tails
- Cracked black pepper
- Olive oil

- Salt to taste

DIRECTIONS:

1. To prepare the lobster tails, lay each tail flat-side down (shell up). Using a sharp knife, cut through the shell and midway through the meat along the length. Use your fingers to pull the meat away from the membranes and the inner shell, then invert the meat until it sits on top of the shell instead of being surrounded by it.
2. Brush the lobster liberally with olive oil and drizzle with black pepper. Put the lemongrass stalks in a Tuscan herb grill.
3. Heat grill to moderate-high heat. Put the herb grill on the main grill grate and put the lobster tails on top, meat side up. Close the lid of the grill and cook for seven to eight minutes. (The shells must be bright red and the meat fairly firm.)
4. Flip the lobster tails over and carry on cooking for two to three minutes.
5. Drizzle with salt before you serve.

GRILLED STEAK WITH PEANUT SAUCE

INGREDIENTS:

- 1 (2-pound) flank steak, trimmed
- 1 recipe of Peanut Dipping Sauce
- 1 recipe of Thai Marinade

DIRECTIONS:

1. Swiftly wash the steak under cold water and pat dry. Put the steak in a big Ziplock bag together with the marinade. Flip the meat until it is thoroughly coated with the marinade on all sides. Place in your fridge overnight.(Allow the steak return to room temperature before cooking.)
2. Preheat a broiler or grill. Cook the steak, flipping over once and coating with the rest of the marinade, until done to your preference
3. Take away the meat from the grill, cover it using foil, and allow it to rest for five minutes to let some of the juices reabsorb. To serve, finely slice the steak across the grain. Pass the peanut sauce separately.

JICAMA, CARROT, AND CHINESE CABBAGE SALAD

Yield: Servings 6–8

INGREDIENTS:

- ½ cup chopped cilantro
- ½ teaspoon prepared chili-garlic sauce
- 1 cup vegetable oil
- 1 teaspoon ground anise
- 2 big carrots, peeled and finely julienned
- 2 pounds jicama, peeled and finely julienned
- 2 tablespoons lime juice
- 3/4 pound Chinese cabbage, thinly shredded
- Salt and black pepper to taste

DIRECTIONS:

1. Thoroughly mix the ground anise, cilantro, vegetable oil, lime juice, and chili-garlic sauce in a big mixing container.
2. Put in the vegetables and toss to coat.
3. Sprinkle with salt and pepper.

LIME BUTTER CAKE

Yield: 1 (12-inch) cake

INGREDIENTS:

- ¼ teaspoon salt
- 1 cup milk
- 1½ cups sugar
- 2 sticks unsalted butter
- 3 cups cake flour
- 3 tablespoons lime juice
- 3 teaspoons baking powder
- 4 eggs, lightly beaten
- Grated peel of 1 lime
- Powdered sugar (not necessary)

DIRECTIONS:

1. Preheat your oven to 325 degrees.
2. Sift together the cake flour, baking powder, and salt three times; set aside.
3. In the container of an electric mixer, beat the butter until creamy.

4. Slowly put in in the sugar, then beat at moderate speed for five minutes, scraping down the sides of the container every so frequently.

5. Put in the beaten eggs slowly and carry on beating for 5 more minutes. (The mixture will be thick and twofold in volume.)

6. Using a rubber spatula, progressively fold in ¼ of the flour mixture into the batter. Then fold in of the milk. Repeat this pulse until all of the flour and the milk have been blended. (You will put in flour last.)

7. Fold in the lime peel and lime juice.

8. Pour the batter into a greased molded cake pan, smoothing the surface and slightly building up the sides.

9. Bake the cake for 45 to 55 minutes or until the top is golden and the sides are starting to pull away from the pan.

10. Take out of the oven and allow to cool for one to two minutes. Cautiously unmold.

11. Allow to cool to room temperature. Sprinkle with powdered sugar or serve with Ginger Anglaise Sauce.

MANY PEAS ASIAN-STYLE SALAD

Yield: Servings 4

INGREDIENTS:

- ½ cup fresh green peas
- ½ cup snow peas
- 1 cup sugar snap peas
- 1 tablespoon brown sugar
- 1 tablespoon rice vinegar
- 1 tablespoon sesame oil
- 2 teaspoons sesame seeds, toasted
- 2 teaspoons soy sauce
- 6 cups pea shoots or other sweet baby lettuce

DIRECTIONS:

1. Bring a big pot of water to its boiling point. Put in the sugar snap peas and boil for a couple of minutes. Put in the snow peas and green peas and boil for a minute more. Drain and wash in cold water. Pat dry using paper towels.

2. In a big container, meticulously mix the sesame seeds, vinegar, oil, sugar, and soy sauce. Put in the peas and the greens and toss to coat.

MARINATED MUSHROOMS

Yield: 25–35

INGREDIENTS:

- ¼ cup rice wine vinegar
- ½ cup water
- ¾ cup olive oil
- 1 whole serrano or jalapeño pepper
- 1½ pounds whole small white mushrooms
- 2 stalks lemongrass
- 3 (½-inch) pieces gingerroot
- 3 cloves garlic
- Juice of 1 lime

DIRECTIONS:

1. Put all of the ingredients apart from the mushrooms in a big pot; bring to its boiling point, reduce heat, and simmer for ten to fifteen minutes.
2. Put in the mushrooms to the pot, stirring to coat.
3. Take away the pot from the heat and let cool completely, approximately 1 hour.
4. Place in your fridge for minimum 2 hours, if possible overnight.

MERINGUES WITH TROPICAL FRUIT

Yield: Approximately 24

INGREDIENTS:

- 2 cups heavy cream, whipped
- 2 cups mixed fresh tropical
- 2 cups superfine sugar
- 6 egg whites
- Butter at room temperature to prepare baking dishes
- fruit, cut into bite-sized pieces

DIRECTIONS:

1. Preheat your oven to 200 degrees. Butter pieces of parchment paper cut to line 2 baking sheets.
2. Put the egg whites in a cold container. Beat until tender peaks form Put in the sugar and carry on beating until firm.
3. Using a pastry bag, pipe 3- to 4-inch circles of meringue onto the readied baking sheets.

4. Bake for 90 to 1twenty minutes or until they are dry, ensuring not to let the meringues turn color. If the meringues aren't dry after 2 hours of baking, turn the oven off and let the meringues sit in your oven overnight.

5. Allow the meringues to cool to room temperature. Fill a pastry bag with the whipped heavy cream. Pipe cream into the center of the meringues. Top with tropical fruit before you serve.

PEANUT-POTATO SALAD

Yield: Servings 8–10

INGREDIENTS:

- ¼ cup chopped cilantro
- ¼ cup chopped mint
- ¼ cup peanut butter
- ¾ cup mayonnaise
- 1 cup salted peanuts, crudely chopped, divided
- 1 moderate-sized red bell pepper, cored and chopped
- 2 stalks celery, cut
- 3 pounds peeled boiling potatoes
- 3 tablespoons rice vinegar
- 4 green onions, trimmed and cut
- Salt and pepper to taste

DIRECTIONS:

1. Bring a big pot of water to its boiling point using high heat. Put in the potatoes and cook until soft. Drain and cool. Cut into ½-inch cubes.

2. In a big container, mix the potato cubes, ¾ cup of peanuts, red bell pepper, celery, green onion, cilantro, and mint.

3. In a small container, whisk together the mayonnaise, peanut butter, and vinegar. Sprinkle salt and pepper to taste.

4. Pour the dressing over the potato mixture and toss to coat. Place in your fridge for minimum 1 hour. Decorate using the rest of the peanuts before you serve.

PICKLED CHINESE CABBAGE

Yield: 3 pounds

INGREDIENTS:

- 1 tablespoon chopped cilantro
- 1 tablespoon chopped garlic
- 2 big shallots or 1 medium onion, chopped
- 3 pounds Chinese cabbage, cored, halved, and thinly cut
- 4 cups water
- 6 cups rice vinegar
- Salt and white pepper

DIRECTIONS:

1. Put all of the ingredients apart from the cabbage in a big stew pot and bring to its boiling point. Decrease the heat and simmer for five minutes.
2. Bring the cooking liquid back to its boiling point and mix in the cabbage. Cover and cook the cabbage for three to five minutes.
3. Take away the pot from heat and let cool completely. Season to taste with salt and white pepper.
4. Place in your fridge for minimum 8 hours before you serve.

SOUTHEAST ASIAN ASPARAGUS

Yield: Servings 4

INGREDIENTS:

- 1 cup toasted peanuts
- 1 pound asparagus, trimmed and slice into two-inch pieces
- 1 tablespoon sesame oil
- 1 teaspoon fish sauce
- 1 teaspoon toasted sesame seeds

DIRECTIONS:

1. Heat the sesame oil in a big frying pan on moderate to high heat. Put in the asparagus and sauté for about three minutes.
2. Put in the fish sauce, sesame seeds, and peanuts. Sauté for two more minutes or until the asparagus is done to your preference.

SOUTHEAST ASIAN BURGERS

Yield: Servings 4

INGREDIENTS:

- ¼ cup chopped basil
- ¼ cup chopped cilantro
- ¼ cup chopped mint
- 1 clove garlic, minced
- 1 pound ground beef or ground turkey
- 1 teaspoon sugar (not necessary)
- 2 tablespoons lime juice
- 3 shakes Tabasco
- 3 tablespoons bread crumbs

DIRECTIONS:

1. In a moderate-sized-sized mixing container, mix all the rest of the ingredients.
2. Use your hands to gently mix the ingredients together and form 4 patties.
3. Season each patty with salt and pepper.
4. Grill the patties to your preference, approximately five minutes per side for medium.

SPICY SHRIMP DIP

Yield: Approximately 1 cup

INGREDIENTS:

- ½ serrano chili, seeded and minced
- ½ teaspoon grated lemon zest
- ½ teaspoon salt
- 1 tablespoon minced chives
- 5 tablespoons butter
- 8 ounces shrimp, cleaned and chopped
- Salt and freshly ground black pepper to taste

DIRECTIONS:

1. In a moderate-sized-sized sauté pan, melt the butter on moderate heat. Mix in the chives, salt, chili pepper, and lemon zest; sauté for a couple of minutes.
2. Lower the heat to low and put in the shrimp; sauté for about three minutes or until opaque.
3. Move the mixture to a food processor and crudely purée. Sprinkle with salt and pepper.
4. Firmly pack the purée into a small container. Cover using plastic wrap, and place in your fridge for 4 hours or overnight.

5. To serve, remove the shrimp dip from the fridge and let it sit for five to ten minutes. Serve the dip with an assortment of crackers and toast points or some favorite veggies.

THAI CHICKEN PIZZA

Yield: 1 large pizza

INGREDIENTS:

- ¼— cup peanut or hot chili oil
- ½ cup crudely chopped dry-roasted peanuts
- 1 cup chopped cilantro leaves
- 1 medium carrot, peeled and crudely grated
- 1 recipe Asian or Thai Marinade
- 1 unbaked pizza crust
- 1½ cups bean sprouts
- 1½ cups fontina cheese
- 1½ cups mozzarella cheese
- 2 whole boneless, skinless chicken breasts, cut in half
- 4 green onions, trimmed and thinly cut

DIRECTIONS:

1. Put the chicken breasts in an ovenproof dish. Pour the marinade over the chicken, flipping to coat completely. Cover and place in your fridge for minimum 8 hours. Allow the chicken to return to room temperature before proceeding.
2. Preheat your oven to 325 degrees. Bake the chicken for thirty to forty minutes or until thoroughly cooked. Take away the chicken from the oven and let cool completely. Shred the chicken into minuscule pieces; set aside.
3. Prepare the pizza dough in accordance with package directions.
4. Brush the dough with some of the oil. Top the oil with the cheeses, leaving a ½-inch rim. Evenly spread the chicken, green onions, carrot, bean sprouts, and peanuts on top of the cheese. Sprinkle a little oil over the top.
5. Bake in accordance with package directions for the crust. Remove from oven, drizzle with cilantro, before you serve.

THAI PASTA SALAD

Yield: Servings 8–12

INGREDIENTS:

- ¼ teaspoon ground ginger
- ½ teaspoon red pepper flakes
- 1 clove garlic, minced
- 1 cup bean sprouts
- 1 cup rice wine vinegar
- 1 tablespoon brown sugar
- 1 tablespoon soy sauce
- 1½ cups thinly cut Napa cabbage or bok choy
- 1½ cups thinly cut red cabbage
- 2 medium carrots, shredded
- 2 tablespoons vegetable oil
- 2 tablespoons water
- 3 green onions, trimmed and thinly cut
- 3 tablespoons smooth peanut butter
- 8 ounces dried bow tie or other bite-sized pasta

DIRECTIONS:

1. Cook the pasta in accordance with package directions. Drain and wash under cold water. Put the pasta in a big mixing container and put in the green onions, carrots, and cabbage.
2. In a small mixing container, meticulously mix all the rest of the ingredients except the sprouts.
3. Pour the dressing over the pasta and vegetables; cover and place in your fridge for minimum 2 hours or overnight.
4. Just before you serve, throw in the bean sprouts.

THAI-FLAVORED GREEN BEANS

Yield: Servings 6–8

INGREDIENTS:

- ½ cup chopped cilantro
- 1 rounded tablespoon shrimp paste
- 2 pounds French or regular green beans, trimmed and slice into bite-sized pieces
- 2 tablespoons vegetable oil
- 2 teaspoons minced garlic
- 3 tablespoons unsalted butter

DIRECTIONS:

1. In a pot big enough to hold all of the beans, steam them until soft-crisp.

2. Drain the beans, saving for later cooking liquid. Cover the beans using foil to keep warm.

3. In a small container, whisk together the shrimp paste and vegetable oil.

4. In a big frying pan, melt the butter on moderate to high heat. Put in the garlic and sauté until golden. Mix in the shrimp paste mixture and 1 tablespoon of the reserved cooking liquid.

5. Put in the reserved green beans, stirring to coat. Cook until thoroughly heated.

6. Take away the pan from the heat and toss in the cilantro.

THAI-SPICED GUACAMOLE

Yield: 2 cups

INGREDIENTS:

- 1 big plum tomato, seeded and chopped
- 1 small garlic clove, minced
- 1 tablespoon chopped onion
- 1 teaspoon chopped serrano or jalapeño chili
- 1 teaspoon grated gingerroot
- 1 teaspoon grated lime zest
- 1–2 tablespoons chopped cilantro
- 2 ripe avocados, pitted and chopped
- 4 teaspoons lime juice
- Salt and freshly ground black pepper to taste

DIRECTIONS:

1. Put the avocado in a moderate-sized container. Put in the lemon juice and crudely mash.

2. Put in the rest of the ingredients and gently mix together.

3. Serve within 2 hours.

THAI-STYLE GRILLED PORK CHOPS

Yield: Servings 2

INGREDIENTS:

- 1 cup fish sauce
- 2 (1-inch-thick) pork chops
- 2 tablespoons cream sherry

- 2 teaspoons brown sugar
- 2 teaspoons minced gingerroot
- 3 tablespoons rice vinegar
- garlic clove, minced

DIRECTIONS:

1. In a small deep cooking pan, on moderate heat, bring the garlic, fish sauce, sherry, vinegar, brown sugar, and gingerroot to its boiling point. Turn off the heat and let cool to room temperature. (You can also put the marinade in your fridge to cool it.)
2. Put the pork chops in a plastic bag and pour in the marinade, ensuring to coat both sides of the chops. Allow the chops marinate at room temperature for fifteen minutes.
3. Pour the marinade into a small deep cooking pan and bring to a simmer on moderate to low heat. Cook for five minutes.
4. Grill the chops on a hot grill for five to six minutes per side for medium.
5. Serve the chops with the marinade sprinkled over the top.

5-SPICED VEGETABLES

Yield: Servings 4–6

INGREDIENTS:

- ¼ teaspoon crushed red pepper flakes
- ½ — ¾ teaspoon Chinese 5-spice powder
- ½ cup orange juice
- 1 cup carrot slices
- 1 pound mushrooms, cut
- 1 small onion, halved and thinly cut
- 1 tablespoon cornstarch
- 1 tablespoon vegetable oil
- 1–2 cloves garlic, minced
- 2 tablespoons soy sauce
- 2 teaspoons honey
- 3 cups broccoli florets

DIRECTIONS:

1. In a small container, mix the orange juice, cornstarch, 5-spice powder, red pepper flakes, soy sauce, and honey; set aside.

2. Heat the vegetable oil in a wok or frying pan on moderate to high heat. Put in the mushrooms, carrots, onion, and garlic. Stir-fry for roughly 4 minutes.

3. Put in the broccoli and carry on cooking an extra 2 to 4 minutes.

4. Mix in the sauce. Cook until the vegetables are done to your preference and the sauce is thick, roughly two minutes.

5. Serve over rice noodles, pasta, or rice.

ALMOND "TEA"

Yield: Servings 4–6

INGREDIENTS:

- ¼–½ cup sugar
- ½ teaspoon ground cardamom
- 2 cups milk
- 2 ounces pumpkin seeds
- 3 cups water
- 3 ounces blanched almonds

DIRECTIONS:

1. Process the almonds, pumpkin seeds, cardamom, and half of the water in a blender or food processor until the solids are thoroughly ground.

2. Strain the almond water through cheesecloth (or a clean Handi Wipe) into a container. Using the back of a spoon, press the solids to remove as much moisture as you can.

3. Return the almond mixture to the blender and put in the remaining water. Process until meticulously blended.

4. Strain this liquid into the container.

5. Mix the milk into the almond water. Put in sugar to taste.

6. Serve over crushed ice.

BANANA BROWN RICE PUDDING

Yield: Servings 4–6

INGREDIENTS:

- ¼ cup water
- ½ teaspoon cinnamon
- ½ teaspoon nutmeg

- 1 (fifteen-ounce) can fruit cocktail, drained
- 1 cup skim milk
- 1 medium banana, cut
- 1 teaspoon vanilla extract
- 1½ cups cooked brown rice
- 2 tablespoons honey

DIRECTIONS:

1. In a moderate-sized-sized deep cooking pan, mix the banana, fruit cocktail, water, honey, vanilla, cinnamon, and nutmeg. Bring to its boiling point on moderate to high heat. Lower the heat and simmer for about ten minutes or until the bananas are soft.
2. Mix in the milk and the rice. Return the mixture to its boiling point, decrease the heat again, and simmer for ten more minutes. Serve warm.

BASIC VIETNAMESE CHILI SAUCE

Yield: Approximately ¼ cup

INGREDIENTS:

- ½ teaspoon brown sugar
- 1 tablespoon lemon juice
- 1 tablespoon rice wine vinegar
- 2 cloves garlic, minced
- 2 dried red chilies, stemmed, seeded, and soaked in hot water until soft
- 2 tablespoons fish sauce

DIRECTIONS:

1. Using a mortar and pestle, grind together the dried chilies and the garlic to make a rough paste.
2. Mix in the sugar until well blended. Mix in the rest of the ingredients.

BEEF CAMBOGEE

Yield: Servings 4–6

INGREDIENTS:

- ½ cup chopped peanuts
- 1 pound sirloin, trimmed, and slice into bite-sized pieces
- 2 cups bean sprouts

- 2–3 moderate-sized russet potatoes, peeled and slice into bite-sized pieces
- 5 cups Red Curry Cambogee (recipe on page 250)

DIRECTIONS:

1. In a big deep cooking pan, bring the curry sauce to a simmer.
2. Put in the meat and potatoes and simmer until done to your preference, approximately twenty minutes to half an hour.
3. Decorate using the peanuts and bean sprouts.

CAMBODIAN BEEF WITH LIME SAUCE

Yield: Servings 4

INGREDIENTS:

- 1 tablespoon sugar
- 1 teaspoon water
- 1½ pounds sirloin, trimmed and slice into bite-sized cubes
- 2 tablespoons lime juice
- 2 tablespoons soy sauce
- 2 tablespoons vegetable oil
- 2 teaspoons freshly ground black pepper, divided
- 5–7 cloves garlic, crushed

DIRECTIONS:

1. In a container big enough to hold the beef, mix the sugar, 1 teaspoon of black pepper, soy sauce, and garlic. Put in the beef and toss to coat. Cover and let marinate for half an hour
2. In a small serving dish, mix the rest of the black pepper, the lime juice, and the water; set aside.
3. In a big sauté pan, heat the vegetable oil on moderate to high heat. Put in the beef cubes and sauté for about four minutes for medium-rare.
4. This dish may be served either as an appetizer or a main dish. For the appetizer, mound the beef on a plate lined with lettuce leaves with the lime sauce on the side. Use toothpicks or small forks to immerse the beef into the lime sauce. For a main dish, toss the beef with the lime sauce to taste. Serve with Jasmine rice.

CAMBODIAN-STYLE PAN-FRIED CHICKEN AND MUSHROOMS

Yield: Servings 4–6

INGREDIENTS:

- ½ teaspoon grated ginger
- 1 cup water
- 1½ pounds chicken breasts and legs
- 2 tablespoons vegetable oil
- 2 teaspoons sugar
- 4 cloves garlic, crushed
- 6 ounces dried Chinese mushrooms

DIRECTIONS:

1. Put the dried mushrooms in a container, cover with boiling water, and allow to soak for half an hour Drain the mushrooms and wash under cold water; drain again and squeeze dry. Remove any tough stems. Chop the mushrooms into bite-sized pieces; set aside.
2. Put the vegetable oil in a wok or big frying pan on moderate to high heat. Put in the garlic and the ginger and stir-fry for a short period of time.
3. Put in the chicken and fry until the skin turns golden.
4. Mix in the water and the sugar. Put in the mushrooms.
5. Lower the heat to low, cover, and cook until the chicken is soft, approximately 30 minutes.

CARDAMOM COOKIES

Yield: 2 dozen cookies

INGREDIENTS:

- ½ cup fine sugar
- 1 cup fine semolina
- 1½ teaspoons ground cardamom
- 3 tablespoons all-purpose flour
- 4 ounces ghee

DIRECTIONS:

1. Preheat your oven to 300 degrees.
2. In a big mixing container, cream together the ghee and the sugar until light and fluffy.
3. Sift together the semolina, all-purpose flour, and cardamom.
4. Mix the dry ingredients into the ghee mixture; mix thoroughly.

5. Allow the dough stand in a cool place for half an hour

6. Form balls using roughly 1 tablespoon of dough for each. Put on an ungreased cookie sheet and flatten each ball slightly.

7. Bake for roughly thirty minutes or until pale brown.

8. Cool on a wire rack. Store in an airtight container.

CHAPATI

Yield: Servings 6–8

INGREDIENTS:

- 1 cup lukewarm water
- 1 tablespoon ghee or oil
- 1½ teaspoons salt
- 3 cups whole-wheat flour

DIRECTIONS:

1. In a big mixing container, mix together 2½ cups of flour and the salt. Put in the ghee and, using your fingers, rub it into the flour and salt mixture.

2. Put in the lukewarm water and mix to make a dough. Knead the dough until it is smooth and elastic, approximately ten minutes. (Do not skimp on the kneading; it is what makes the bread soft.)

3. Form the dough into a ball and put it in a small, oiled container. Cover firmly using plastic wrap and allow it to rest at room temperature for minimum 1 hour.

4. Split the dough into golf ball–sized pieces. Using a flour-covered rolling pin, roll each ball out on a flour-covered surface to roughly 6 to 8 inches in diameter and -inch thick.

5. Heat a big frying pan or griddle on moderate heat. Put a piece of dough on the hot surface. Using a towel or the edge of a spoon, cautiously press down around the edges of the bread. (This will allow air pockets to make in the bread.) Cook for a minute. Cautiously turn the chapati over and carry on cooking for 1 more minute. Chapatis must be mildly browned and flexible, not crunchy. Take away the bread to a basket and cover using a towel. Repeat until all of the rounds are cooked.

CHILIED COCONUT DIPPING SAUCE

Yield: Approximately 1 cup

INGREDIENTS:

- ¼ cup fresh coconut juice
- 1 serrano chili, seeded and minced

- 1 tablespoon lime juice

- 1 teaspoon rice wine vinegar

- 1 teaspoon sugar

- 2 cloves garlic, minced

- 2 tablespoons fish sauce

DIRECTIONS:

1. Bring the coconut juice, rice wine vinegar, and sugar to its boiling point in a small deep cooking pan. Turn off the heat and allow the mixture to cool completely.

2. Mix in the rest of the ingredients.

CUCUMBER RAITA

Yield: Approximately 4 cups

INGREDIENTS:

- 1 teaspoon salt

- 1½ cups plain yogurt

- 1–2 green onions, trimmed and thinly cut

- 2 seedless cucumbers, peeled and slice into a small dice

- 2 tablespoons fresh mint

- Lemon juice to taste

DIRECTIONS:

1. Put the diced cucumbers in a colander. Drizzle with salt and allow it to sit in the sink for fifteen minutes to drain. Wash the cucumber under cold water and drain once more.

2. Mix the cucumber, yogurt, green onions, mint, and lemon juice to taste.

3. Cover and place in your fridge for minimum 30 minutes. Check seasoning, putting in additional salt and/or lemon juice if required.

FRUIT IN SHERRIED SYRUP

Yield: Servings 4–6

INGREDIENTS:

- 1 orange, peeled and segmented

- 1½ cups kiwi slices

- 2 cups fresh pineapple chunks

- 2 tablespoons dry sherry
- 2 tablespoons sugar
- 2 teaspoons lemon juice
- 4 tablespoons water

DIRECTIONS:

1. In a small deep cooking pan using high heat, boil the sugar and the water until syrupy. Turn off the heat and let cool completely. Mix in the lemon juice and sherry; set aside.
2. In a serving container, mix the orange segments, the pineapple chunks, and the kiwi. Pour the syrup over the fruit and toss to blend. Place in your fridge for minimum 1 hour before you serve.

GARAM MASALA

Yield: Approximately 1 cup

INGREDIENTS:

- 1 tablespoon whole black peppercorns
- 1 teaspoon whole cloves
- 2 small cinnamon sticks, broken into pieces
- 2 tablespoons cumin seeds
- 2 teaspoons cardamom seeds
- 4 tablespoons coriander seeds

DIRECTIONS:

1. In a small heavy sauté pan, individually dry roast each spice on moderate to high heat until they start to release their aroma.
2. Allow the spices to cool completely and then put them in a spice grinder and process to make a quite fine powder.
3. Store in an airtight container.

HAPPY PANCAKES

Yield: Servings 4

INGREDIENTS:

- ¼ cup mixed, chopped herbs (mint, cilantro, basil, etc.)
- ¼ teaspoon salt

- ½ cup bean sprouts
- ½ cup finely cut straw mushrooms, washed and patted dry
- 1 cup rice flour
- 1 tablespoon vegetable oil
- 1 teaspoon sugar
- 1½ cups water
- 2 eggs, lightly beaten
- 3 ounces cooked salad shrimp, washed and patted dry
- Chili dipping sauce

DIRECTIONS:

1. In a moderate-sized-sized container, whisk together the rice flour, water, eggs, salt, and sugar. Set aside and let the batter rest for about ten minutes.
2. Strain the batter through a mesh sieve to remove any lumps.
3. Put in the vegetable oil to a big sauté or omelet pan. Heat on high until super hot, but not smoking.
4. Pour the batter into the hot pan, swirling it so that it coats the bottom of the pan uniformly. Drizzle the mushrooms over the batter. Cover and allow to cook for a minute.
5. Drizzle the shrimp and bean sprouts uniformly over the pancake. Carry on cooking until the bottom is crunchy and browned.
6. To serve, chop the pancake into four equivalent portions. Drizzle with the chopped herbs. Pass a favorite dipping sauce separately.

HONEYED CHICKEN

Yield: Servings 3–4

INGREDIENTS:

- ½ teaspoon Chinese 5-spice powder
- 1 (1-inch) piece ginger, peeled and minced
- 1 medium onion, peeled and slice into wedges
- 1 pound boneless, skinless chicken breasts, cut into bite-sized pieces
- 2 tablespoons fish sauce
- 2 tablespoons honey
- 2 tablespoons soy sauce
- 2 tablespoons vegetable oil
- 3–4 cloves garlic, thinly cut

DIRECTIONS:

1. Mix the honey, fish sauce, soy sauce, and 5-spice powder in a small container; set aside.

2. Heat the oil in a wok on moderate to high. Put in the onion and cook until it just starts to brown.

3. Put in the chicken; stir-fry for three to four minutes.

4. Put in the garlic and ginger, and continue stir-frying for 30 more seconds.

5. Mix in the honey mixture and allow to cook for three to four minutes, until the chicken is glazed and done to your preference.

HOT NOODLES WITH TOFU

Yield: Servings 4

INGREDIENTS:

*   ½ pound Chinese wheat noodles
*   ½ pound dried tofu, soaked in hot water for fifteen minutes and slice into 1-inch cubes
*   ½ pound firm tofu, cut into 1-inch cubes
*   ½ teaspoon yellow asafetida powder
*   1 bunch choy sum, chopped into 1-inch pieces
*   2 cups mung bean shoots or bean sprouts
*   3 tablespoons lemon juice
*   3 tablespoons minced ginger
*   3 tablespoons sambal oelek
*   3 tablespoons sesame oil
*   3 tablespoons soy sauce
*   Vegetable oil for frying

DIRECTIONS:

1. Cook the noodles firm to the bite in accordance with package directions. Wash under cold water and drain; set aside.

2. Heat approximately two inches of vegetable oil in a wok or big frying pan over moderate high heat. Put in the firm tofu cubes and deep-fry until golden. Using a slotted spoon, remove the tofu cubes to paper towels to drain; set aside.

3. Put in the dried tofu pieces and deep-fry them until they blister. Remove and drain using paper towels; set aside.

4. In another wok or frying pan heat the sesame oil using high heat. Put in the ginger and stir-fry one minute.

5. Put in the asafetida and choy sum, and stir-fry until tender.

6. Mix in the soy sauce, sambal oelek, and lemon juice. Put in the noodles and tofu pieces. Stir-fry until hot, approximately 2 minutes more.

INDIAN-SCENTED CAULIFLOWER

Yield: Servings 2–4

INGREDIENTS:

- ½ medium to big head of cauliflower, separated into florets and slice into pieces
- ½ teaspoon Garam Masala
- ½ teaspoon turmeric
- 1 (2-inch) piece ginger, peeled and minced
- 1 clove garlic, minced
- 1 teaspoon mustard seeds
- 1 teaspoon salt
- 3 tablespoons vegetable oil
- 3 tablespoons water

DIRECTIONS:

1. In a deep cooking pan big enough to easily hold the cauliflower, heat the vegetable oil on moderate to high heat. Put in the mustard seeds and fry until they pop. Put in the garlic and the ginger; stirring continuously, cook until the garlic just starts to brown.

2. Mix in the turmeric. Put in the cauliflower pieces and toss to coat with the spice mixture.

3. Put in the water, cover, and allow to steam for 6 to ten minutes or until done to your preference.

4. Pour off any surplus water and drizzle with the garam masala.

MANGO CHUTNEY

Yield: Approximately 5–6 cups

INGREDIENTS:

- ½ ounce golden raisins
- ½ teaspoon black mustard seeds
- 1 cup water
- 1 tablespoon chopped ginger
- 1 tablespoon minced garlic
- 1 teaspoon cumin

- 1–2 red chili peppers, seeded and minced
- 2 big green mangoes, peeled and cut
- 2 cups sugar
- 2 cups white vinegar
- 2 teaspoons Garam Masala
- 3 teaspoons salt
- 4 ounces dried apricots or cherries

DIRECTIONS:

1. Put all of the ingredients in a heavy-bottomed deep cooking pan. Heat to a simmer on moderate heat, stirring until the sugar dissolves.
2. Simmer for thirty minutes or until thick.
3. Seal in airtight jars.

MINTED VEGETABLES

Yield: Servings 6

INGREDIENTS:

- ½ cup vegetable broth
- 1 medium onion, cut into 1-inch pieces
- 1 red bell pepper, seeded and slice into 1-inch pieces
- 2 teaspoons vegetable oil, divided
- 3 cups broccoli pieces
- 3 cups thinly cut red cabbage
- 3–4 tablespoons chopped mint
- 4 medium carrots, peeled and slice into thin slices
- Salt and pepper to taste

DIRECTIONS:

1. In a big frying pan, heat 1 teaspoon of vegetable oil on moderate to high heat. Put in the carrot slices, onion, and bell pepper; sauté for five minutes.
2. Put in the remaining teaspoon of oil, the broccoli, the cabbage, and the vegetable broth. Continue to sauté until the vegetables are done to your preference, approximately ten minutes for soft-crisp.
3. Sprinkle salt and pepper to taste. Mix in the chopped mint.

MULLIGATAWNY SOUP

Yield: Servings 8–10

INGREDIENTS:

- 1 (1½-inch) cinnamon stick
- 1 (14-ounce) can coconut milk
- 1 jalapeño, seeded and cut
- 1 tablespoon ground cumin
- 1 tablespoon vegetable oil
- 2 medium onions, peeled
- 2 tablespoons ground coriander
- 2 teaspoons salt
- 2 teaspoons whole peppercorns
- 3 cloves garlic, peeled
- 3 pounds chicken wings
- 4 whole cloves
- 4–5 cups cooked rice
- 5 cardamom pods, bruised
- 6 cups chicken broth
- 8–12 fresh curry leaves
- Lemon juice to taste

DIRECTIONS:

1. Put the chicken wings in a big soup pot. Cover the chicken with cold water.
2. Stick the cloves into 1 of the onions and put the onion in the pot with the chicken.
3. Put in the garlic, jalapeño, cinnamon stick, peppercorns, cardamom, coriander, cumin, and salt; bring the mixture to its boiling point, reduce to a simmer, and cook for two to three hours.
4. Allow the stock come to room temperature. Take away the chicken pieces from the broth and chop the meat from the bones. Set aside the meat.
5. Strain the broth.
6. Thinly slice the rest of the onion.
7. In a big sauté pan, heat the oil on moderate to high heat. Put in the onion slices and sauté until translucent. Put in the curry leaves and the broth. Heat to a simmer and allow to cook for five minutes.

8. Put in enough water to the coconut milk to make 3 cups of liquid. Put in this and the reserved meat to the broth. Heat the soup, but do not allow it to boil. Season to taste with additional salt and a squeeze of lemon juice.

9. To serve, place roughly ½ cup of cooked rice on the bottom of each container. Ladle the soup over the rice.

OYSTER MUSHROOM SOUP

Yield: Servings 4

INGREDIENTS:

- ½ pound oyster mushrooms, cleaned and separated if large
- ½ stalk lemongrass, outer leaves removed, inner core finely chopped
- 1 tablespoon Tabasco
- 1 teaspoon sugar
- 2 tablespoons lemon juice
- 2–3 serrano chilies
- 3 (2-inch-long, ½-inch wide) pieces lime zest
- 4 cups vegetable broth

DIRECTIONS:

1. In a big deep cooking pan, bring the vegetable broth and the Tabasco to its boiling point. In the meantime, crush the chilies with a mallet to break them slightly open: A good whack will do it.

2. Put in all of the rest of the ingredients to the boiling broth, reduce the heat, and simmer until the mushrooms are cooked to your preference. Take away the chilies before you serve.

PENINSULA SWEET POTATOES

Yield: Servings 4

INGREDIENTS:

- ¼ teaspoon salt
- 1 (14-ounce) can coconut milk
- 1 bay leaf
- 1 pound sweet potatoes or yams of varying varieties, peeled and slice into bite-sized pieces
- 1 teaspoon sugar

DIRECTIONS:

1. Put the sweet potato pieces in a big deep cooking pan. Put in barely sufficient water to cover them, and bring to its boiling point. Put in the bay leaf and cook until the potatoes are tender. Take away the bay leaf and discard.

2. Mix in the sugar and salt. After the sugar has dissolved, remove the pan from the heat and mix in the coconut milk. Tweak the seasonings by putting in salt and/or sugar if required. Adjust the consistency by putting in more water and/or coconut milk.

PORK MEDALLIONS IN A CLAY POT

Yield: Servings 4

INGREDIENTS:

- ½ teaspoon ground black pepper
- 1 clove garlic, minced
- 1 cup water
- 1 tablespoon Black Bean Paste (Page 10)
- 1 tablespoon cornstarch
- 1 tablespoon Tamarind Concentrate (Page 20)
- 1 teaspoon rice wine
- 1 teaspoon sesame oil
- 2 pork tenderloins, trimmed and slice into ½-inch slices
- 2 tablespoons light soy sauce
- 2 tablespoons oyster sauce
- 2 tablespoons sweet (dark) soy sauce
- 2 tablespoons vegetable oil

DIRECTIONS:

1. Prepare the marinade by combining the oyster sauce, light and dark soy sauces, Black Bean Paste, sesame oil, rice wine, black pepper, garlic, and cornstarch in a moderate-sized container.

2. Put in the pork slices to the container of marinade and toss to coat completely. Cover the pork and let marinate at room temperature for half an hour

3. Heat the vegetable oil in a wok on moderate to high heat. Put in the marinated pork and stir-fry for three to four minutes.

4. Move the pork to a clay pot or other ovenproof braising vessel.

5. Mix together the tamarind and water; pour over the pork.

6. Bake the pork in a 350-degree oven for about ninety minutes, until super soft.

POTATO SAMOSAS

Yield: 20 samosas

INGREDIENTS:

For the crust:
- ½ teaspoon salt
- 1½ cups all-purpose flour
- 4 tablespoons butter, at room temperature
- Ice water
- Vegetable oil for deep frying

For the filling:
- ¼ pound sweet peas, thawed if frozen
- ½ teaspoon chili powder
- ½ teaspoon turmeric
- 1 tablespoon ghee (see note) or oil
- 1 teaspoon salt
- 1¼ pounds russet potatoes, peeled
- 2 jalapeños, seeded and thinly cut
- 2 teaspoons mustard seeds
- 3 tablespoons chopped mint
- Lemon juice to taste

DIRECTIONS:
1. To make the pastry crust: In a big container, sift together the flour and the salt. Using a pastry cutter, chop the butter into the flour mixture.
2. Put in the ice water, 1 tablespoon at a time, until a firm dough is achieved. You will probably use 5 to 6 tablespoons of water total. Knead the dough for roughly five minutes or until it is smooth and elastic. Put the dough in an oiled container, cover using plastic wrap, and set it aside while making the potato filling.
3. To make the filling: Bring a big pan of water to its boiling point. Put in the potatoes and cook until fairly soft. Drain the potatoes and let them cool until they are easy to handle. Cut them into a small dice; set aside.

4. In a big frying pan, heat the ghee on moderate to high heat. Put in the mustard seeds and sauté until the seeds start to pop. Mix in the turmeric and the chili powder; cook for fifteen seconds. Mix in the potatoes, peas, salt, and jalapeño slices. (It is okay if the potatoes and the peas get a little smashed.) Turn off the heat, mix in the mint and lemon juice to taste, and save for later.

5. Roll the pastry until it is fairly thin (-inch thick). Cut roughly ten 6-inch circles from the dough. Cut each circle in half. Put a loaded tablespoon of filling in the middle of each half circle. Dampen the edges of the dough with cold water, fold the dough over on itself to make a triangle, and seal tightly.

6. To fry, put in roughly 3 inches of vegetable oil to a big deep cooking pan. Heat the oil using high heat until super hot, but not smoking. Put in the samosas to the hot oil a few at a time and deep-fry until a golden-brown colour is achieved. Using a slotted spoon, remove the samosas to a stack of paper towels to drain.

7. Serve the samosas with Tamarind Dipping Sauce .

PUNJAB FISH

INGREDIENTS:

- ¼ teaspoon cinnamon
- ¼ teaspoon saffron strands, toasted and crushed
- ½ cup plain yogurt
- 1 (1-inch) piece ginger, peeled and minced
- 1 clove garlic, chopped
- 1 medium onion, thinly cut
- 1 teaspoon black pepper
- 1 teaspoon salt
- 1 teaspoon turmeric
- 2 serrano chilies, seeded and minced
- 2 tablespoons almond slivers
- 2 tablespoons boiling water
- 2 teaspoons cardamom
- 2 teaspoons cumin
- 2–3 tablespoons vegetable oil
- 4–6 firm-fleshed fish fillets, roughly 1-inch thick
- Lemon juice
- teaspoon ground cloves

DIRECTIONS:

1. Wash the fish with cold water and pat dry. Rub the fish with lemon juice.

2. Mix the salt, pepper, and turmeric; drizzle over the fish.

3. Heat one to 2 tablespoons of vegetable oil in a big frying pan using high heat. Brown the fish swiftly on each side. Take away the fish to a plate, cover, and save for later.

4. Put in the onion to the same pan and sauté until translucent and just starting to brown.

5. Put the cooked onion in a food processor together with the garlic, ginger, chilies, and almonds. Process to make a paste, putting in a small amount of water if required. Put in the cumin, cardamom, cinnamon, and clove; process to meticulously blend.

6. If required, put in additional vegetable oil to the frying pan to make about 2 tablespoons. Heat the oil over moderate. Put in the spice mixture and cook, stirring continuously, for approximately 2 minutes. Swirl a small amount of water in the food processor to remove any remaining spices and pour it into the pan; stir until blended.

7. Pour 2 tablespoons of boiling water into a small cup. Put in the toasted saffron and stir until blended. Pour the saffron water into the frying pan.

8. Mix in the yogurt. Heat to a simmer and allow the sauce to cook for five minutes.

9. Put in the fish to the sauce, flipping to coat. Cover and allow to simmer for roughly ten minutes or until the fish is done to your preference.

RED CURRY CAMBOGEE

Yield: Approximately 4½ cups

This Cambodian sauce is a hotter version of the Lemongrass Curry Sauce. It makes a great base for beef dishes.

INGREDIENTS:

*   1 cup boiling water
*   2 tablespoons vegetable oil
*   4 cups Lemongrass Curry Sauce
*   4 dried Thai bird chilies, stemmed and seeded
*   4 tablespoons sweet paprika

DIRECTIONS:

1. Break the dried chilies into pieces and put them in a small container. Cover with the boiling water and allow it to sit until soft, approximately fifteen minutes.

2. Put the chilies, their steeping water, and the paprika in a blender. Process to make a thin paste.

3. Heat the vegetable oil on moderate to high heat in a wok. Put in the chili paste and stir-fry until it starts to darken. Turn off the heat and save for later.

4. Put the Lemongrass Curry Sauce in a moderate-sized deep cooking pan. Mix in half of the chili paste and bring to its boiling point. Lower the heat and allow to simmer for five to ten minutes. Check the flavor of the sauce, putting in more chili paste if required.

LEMONGRASS CURRY SAUCE

Yield: Approximately 4 cups

INGREDIENTS:

- 1 cup chopped lemongrass, inner core only
- 1 teaspoon minced ginger
- 1 teaspoon turmeric
- 1 jalapeño chili, stemmed and seeded
- 3 small shallots, crudely chopped
- 3 (14-ounce) cans coconut milk
- 3 (2-inch-long, ½-inch wide) pieces lime peel
- ¼ teaspoon salt
- 4–5 cloves garlic, chopped

DIRECTIONS:

1. Put the lemongrass, garlic, ginger, turmeric, chili, and shallots in a food processor; process to make a paste.

2. Bring the coconut milk to its boiling point and put in the lemongrass paste, lime peel, and salt. Decrease the heat and allow to simmer for 30 to forty-five minutes. Take away the lime peel.

ROASTED DUCK, MELON, AND MANGO SALAD

Yield: Servings 4–6

INGREDIENTS:

- ½ big cucumber, seeded and cut
- ½ roast duck, meat removed and shredded
- ½ teaspoon granulated salt
- ½ teaspoon sesame oil
- 1 cup cubed cantaloupe

- 1 cup cubed honeydew melon
- 1 cup cubed jicama
- 1 mango, cut into bite-sized pieces
- 1 pear, cut into bite-sized pieces
- 1 tablespoon plus 2 teaspoons vegetable oil
- 1 teaspoon bottled chili sauce
- 1 teaspoon ketchup
- 1 teaspoon oyster sauce
- 1 teaspoon soy sauce
- 1 teaspoon sugar
- 1½ teaspoons apricot jam
- 1½ teaspoons cornstarch
- 2 tablespoons toasted sesame seeds
- 2 teaspoons fine sugar
- 3 tablespoons ground peanuts
- 3 tablespoons water

DIRECTIONS:

1. In a moderate-sized-sized mixing container, mix the soy sauce, fine sugar, oyster sauce, and 1 tablespoon of the vegetable oil. Put in the shredded duck to the container and toss to coat; set aside.

2. In a small container, whisk together the 3 tablespoons of water, salt, 1 teaspoon of sugar, sesame oil, ketchup, chili sauce, and cornstarch; set aside.

3. In a small deep cooking pan, heat the rest of the vegetable oil on moderate heat. Put in the sauce mixture to the pan and cook until it becomes thick. Mix in the apricot jam and remove the pan from the heat. Cool the sauce in your fridge. Stir before you use.

4. Mound the duck in the middle of a big serving platter. Position the fruits and vegetables around the duck. Ladle the sauce over the duck, fruits, and vegetables. Drizzle the salad with chopped peanuts and sesame seeds. Serve immediately.

SHRIMP "PÂTÉ"

Yield: Servings 4

INGREDIENTS:

- ¼ teaspoon white pepper
- ½ teaspoon salt

- 1 red chili, seeded and thoroughly minced (not necessary)
- 1 teaspoon sugar
- 1¼ cups minced shrimp
- 2 tablespoons vegetable oil
- 8 (4-inch) pieces sugarcane Sweet-and-sour or other favorite dipping sauce

DIRECTIONS:

1. Preheat your oven to 375 degrees.
2. Put the shrimp, salt, sugar, white pepper, and chili in a food processor; process until the desired smoothness is achieved.
3. Sprinkle in one to 2 tablespoons of the vegetable oil. Process the shrimp mixture until it reaches the consistency necessary to make a meatball, using nearly oil.
4. Split the shrimp mixture into 4 equivalent portions.
5. Use your hands to mold a "shrimp ball" around the center of each of the sugarcane pieces.
6. Put the "skewers" on a baking sheet and roast for roughly twenty minutes. If you prefer them a little extra browned, broil them (after they are done baking) until the desired color is reached.
7. To serve, spoon some of the sweet-and-sour sauce into the middle of 4 plates. Put the sugarcane "skewer" on top of the sauce.

SINGAPORE NOODLES

Yield: Servings 2–3

INGREDIENTS:

- ¼ cup oyster sauce
- 1 package rice sticks, soaked in hot water until tender and drained
- 1–2 teaspoons red pepper flakes
- 2 cups cooked meat or shrimp in bite-sized pieces
- 2 green onions, trimmed and thinly cut
- 2 tablespoons minced ginger
- 2 tablespoons vegetable oil
- 2 teaspoons soy sauce
- 3 tablespoons curry powder
- 4 cloves garlic, minced

DIRECTIONS:

1. Heat the vegetable oil in a wok or big frying pan on moderate to high heat. Put in the garlic and the ginger. Stir-fry until tender.
2. Put in the cooked meat or shrimp, green onion, and red pepper flakes to the wok; stir-fry until hot.
3. Mix in the oyster sauce, curry powder, and soy sauce. Put in the rice noodles and toss. Serve instantly.

SINGAPORE SHELLFISH SOUP

Yield: Servings 6–8

INGREDIENTS:

- ¼ cup chopped cilantro
- 1 (14-ounce) can coconut milk
- 1 (1-inch) piece ginger, peeled and chopped
- 1 7-ounce package of rice noodles, soaked in hot water until soft
- 1 cup bean sprouts
- 1 pound big raw shrimp, peeled, shells reserved
- 1 pound mussels, cleaned and debearded
- 1 tablespoon anchovy paste
- 1 tablespoon ground coriander
- 1 tablespoon lime zest
- 1 teaspoon turmeric
- 1–2 tablespoons fish sauce
- 2 cloves garlic, minced
- 2 tablespoons vegetable oil, divided
- 3 serrano chilies, seeded and chopped
- 3 stalks lemongrass, outer layers removed, inner core thinly cut
- 4 small shallots, peeled and cut
- 6 big scallops, cut horizontally into 2–3 pieces, depending on their size
- Lime wedges

DIRECTIONS:

1. In a moderate-sized-sized deep cooking pan heat 1 tablespoon of the oil on moderate to high heat and fry the shrimp shells until pink.
2. Put in 3 cups of water to the pan and bring to its boiling point; decrease the heat and simmer for half an hour Strain the shells from the broth, then boil the broth until it is reduced to 2 cups.

3. In a big frying pan, bring ½ cup of water to its boiling point. Put in the mussels, cover, and allow to steam until opened, approximately five minutes. Discard any mussels that have not opened. Strain the cooking liquid and save for later. Shell all but about of the mussels; set the mussels aside.

4. Put the lemongrass, chilies, garlic, ginger, shallots, anchovy paste, and 2 tablespoons of water in a food processor. Process to make a thick paste, putting in more water if required.

5. Heat the rest of the vegetable oil in a big soup pot on moderate heat. Put in the lemongrass paste and fry, stirring constantly, until mildly browned, approximately ten minutes. Mix in the turmeric and ground coriander and cook for a minute more.

6. Put in the shrimp broth and mussel cooking liquid to the pot, stirring to dissolve the paste. Bring to its boiling point, reduce heat, and simmer for ten to fifteen minutes.

7. Put in the coconut milk and fish sauce; return to its boiling point. Put in the noodles and lime zest; simmer for a couple of minutes. Put in the shrimp and simmer for a couple of minutes more. Put in the scallop slices. After half a minute or so, put in the shelled mussels and bean sprouts. Lightly stir until blended.

8. To serve, ladle the soup into deep soup bowls. Decorate using the mussels in their shells, drizzle with chopped cilantro and the juice from a lime wedge over the top of each container.

SINGAPORE SHRIMP

Yield: Servings 4

INGREDIENTS:

- ¼ cup green onion slices
- ¼ teaspoon Chinese 5-spice powder
- 1 can coconut milk
- 1 clove garlic, minced
- 1 cup cut domestic mushrooms
- 1 teaspoon minced ginger
- 1½ pounds cooked shrimp
- 2 tablespoons vegetable oil
- 2 teaspoons hoisin sauce
- 2 teaspoons oyster sauce
- 2 teaspoons Red Curry Paste (Page 17)
- Salt and pepper to taste

DIRECTIONS:

1. In a wok or big sauté pan, heat the vegetable oil on moderate to high.

2. Put in the mushrooms, green onions, garlic, and ginger; stir-fry for two to three minutes.

3. Mix together the hoisin sauce, oyster sauce, and curry paste, and 5-spice powder until well blended. Put in the mixture to the wok.

4. Mix in the coconut milk and tweak seasoning to taste with the salt and pepper. Put in the shrimp and bring to a simmer. Cook for one to two minutes until the shrimp are thoroughly heated.

SPICE-POACHED CHICKEN

Yield: Servings 4–6

INGREDIENTS:

- ¼ cup light soy sauce
- ¼ teaspoon dried tangerine peel (dried orange peel can be substituted)
- ½ teaspoon whole black peppercorns
- ½ teaspoon whole cloves
- 1 (2-inch) cinnamon stick
- 1 cardamom pod
- 1 whole star anise
- 2 tablespoons sugar
- 4–6 boneless, skinless chicken breasts
- 5 cups water

DIRECTIONS:

1. Put the star anise, peppercorns, cloves, cinnamon stick, cardamom pod, tangerine peel, and water in a stew pot. Bring the mixture to its boiling point using high heat. Let boil until the poaching liquid is reduced to 4 cups.

2. Mix in the soy sauce and the sugar. Return the liquid to its boiling point.

3. Put in the chicken breasts and reduce to a simmer. Poach the breasts until done, approximately twenty minutes.

SWEET CAMBODIAN BROTH WITH PORK AND EGGS

Yield: Servings 4–6

INGREDIENTS:

- ½ teaspoon freshly ground black pepper
- ½ teaspoon salt
- 1 big pork tenderloin, cut into bite-sized cubes
- 1 cup fish sauce
- 1 cup sugar
- 1 cup thinly cut bamboo shoots
- 4 cups water
- 5 tablespoons soy sauce
- 6–8 hard-boiled eggs
- Rice, cooked in accordance with package directions

DIRECTIONS:

1. Bring the water to its boiling point in a big deep cooking pan. Put in the soy sauce, black pepper, salt, sugar, fish sauce, and hard-boiled eggs; simmer for fifteen minutes.
2. Put in the cubed pork and the bamboo shoots and simmer for another thirty minutes.
3. Lower the heat to low, cover, and allow to simmer for two to three hours. Adjust seasonings to taste.
4. To serve, mound some rice on the bottom of soup bowls. Ladle soup over the rice.

SWEET-AND-SOUR VEGETABLES

Yield: Servings 6

INGREDIENTS:

- ¼ cup rice vinegar
- 1 big green pepper, seeded and slice into bite-sized pieces
- 1 cup brown sugar
- 1 cup cut carrots
- 1 cup fresh pineapple chunks
- 1 cup unsweetened pineapple juice
- 1 cup water, divided
- 1 onion, cut
- 1 teaspoon grated ginger
- 2 cloves garlic, crushed
- 2 tablespoons cornstarch
- 2 tablespoons soy sauce
- 4 cups broccoli

- 6 green onions, trimmed and slice into 1-inch lengths

DIRECTIONS:

1. Put the carrots, onion, green pepper, garlic, and ginger in a big deep cooking pan with ½ cup of the water. Bring the water to its boiling point and allow to cook for five minutes, stirring regularly.

2. Put in the broccoli, green onions, and the rest of the ½ cup of water. Bring the water to its boiling point; reduce the heat, cover, and allow to simmer for five minutes.

3. In the meantime, in a small container, meticulously mix the pineapple juice, rice vinegar, soy sauce, brown sugar, and cornstarch.

4. Put in the pineapple juice mixture and the pineapple chunks to the wok. Raise the heat to moderate and cook, stirring continuously, until the sauce becomes thick.

TAMARIND DIPPING SAUCE

Yield: Approximately 1¼ cups

INGREDIENTS:

- ½ teaspoon ground fennel
- 1 cup hot water
- 1 teaspoon ground cumin
- 1 teaspoon salt
- 2 teaspoons brown sugar
- 2 teaspoons grated ginger
- 3 tablespoons tamarind pulp
- Lemon juice to taste

DIRECTIONS:

1. Put the tamarind pulp in a small container. Pour boiling water over the pulp and allow to soak until soft, approximately fifteen minutes.

2. Break up the pulp and then strain the tamarind water through a fine-mesh sieve, using the back of a spoon to push the pulp through, but leaving the tough fibers.

3. Mix in the rest of the ingredients and let the tamarind sauce sit for minimum fifteen minutes before you serve.

TANDOORI CHICKEN

Yield: Servings 4

INGREDIENTS:

- ½ cup plain yogurt
- ½ teaspoon saffron threads
- 1 tablespoon grated ginger
- 1½ teaspoons Garam Masala
- 2 small garlic cloves, minced
- 2 tablespoons ghee, melted
- 2 teaspoons paprika
- 2 teaspoons salt
- 4 skinless chicken breasts
- 4 skinless chicken legs
- teaspoon chili powder

DIRECTIONS:

1. Using a small, sharp knife, make three to 4 (¼-inch-deep) slits in each piece of chicken. Set aside in a container big enough to hold all of the pieces.
2. Put the saffron in a small sauté pan on moderate heat and toast for roughly half a minute. Put the saffron on a small plate and let it cool and crumble.
3. Mix the saffron into the yogurt.
4. Grind together the ginger, garlic, garlic, salt, chili pepper, paprika, and garam masala. Mix the spice mixture into the yogurt.
5. Pour the yogurt over the chicken, ensuring that all of the pieces are coated. Cover and marinate overnight flipping the pieces in the marinade every so frequently.
6. Preheat your oven to 450 degrees.
7. Put in the ghee to a roasting pan big enough to hold al of the chicken pieces. Put in the chicken, breast side down. Ladle some of the ghee over the pieces. Roast for about ten minutes. Turn the pieces over, coat again, and continue roasting for five minutes. Turn them again and roast for another five minutes. Turn 1 last time (breasts must be up); coat and cook until done, approximately 5 more minutes.

TEA-SMOKED CHICKEN

Yield: Servings 6–8

INGREDIENTS:

- ½ cup brown sugar
- ½ cup cooked rice

- ½ cup green tea leaves
- ½ teaspoon salt
- 1 teaspoon sesame oil
- 2 teaspoons rice wine
- 6–8 boneless, skinless chicken breasts

DIRECTIONS:

1. Swiftly wash the chicken breasts under cold water and pat dry. Drizzle with the salt and rice wine. Set aside in your fridge for half an hour

2. In the meantime, prepare the wok: Coat the bottom using a sheet of aluminium foil. Put the tea leaves, brown sugar, and rice on the bottom of the wok and toss to blend. Place a wire grill rack on the wok.

3. Heat the wok on moderate to high heat. Place the chicken on the rack and cover with a tight-fitting lid. Remove the heat after smoke starts to emit from the wok, but leave it on the burner for about ten minutes or until the chicken is thoroughly cooked.

4. Brush the chicken with the sesame oil. Serve immediately.

TROPICAL FRUITS WITH CINNAMON AND LIME

Yield: Servings 6–12

INGREDIENTS:

- ½ teaspoon sesame oil
- ½–1 teaspoon cinnamon Pinch of salt
- 3 tablespoons honey
- 6 cups of tropical fruits, such as mango, papaya, bananas, melons, star fruit, kiwi, etc., (anything really) cut into bite-sized pieces
- Zest and juice of 6 limes

DIRECTIONS:

1. Mix the lime zest and all but about of the lime juice in a small container. Slowly sprinkle in the honey, whisking to make a smooth mixture. Whisk in the sesame oil, cinnamon, and salt. Adjust flavor to your preference with more lime juice if required.

2. Put the fruit in a big serving container. Pour the cinnamon-lime dressing over the fruit, toss to blend, and allow to rest in your fridge for fifteen minutes before you serve.

VIETNAMESE BANANAS

INGREDIENTS:

- 1 tablespoon grated ginger Grated zest of 1 orange
- 3 tablespoons brown sugar
- 3 tablespoons butter
- 3 tablespoons shredded coconut (unsweetened)
- 3 teaspoons toasted sesame seeds
- 4 tablespoons lime juice
- 6 bananas, peeled and cut in half along the length
- 6 tablespoons orange liqueur

DIRECTIONS:

1. Heat a small nonstick pan using high heat. Put in the coconut and cook, stirring continuously, until a golden-brown colour is achieved. Take away the coconut from the pan and save for later.
2. In a big sauté pan, melt the butter on moderate to high heat. Mix in the brown sugar, the ginger, and orange zest. Put the bananas in the pan, cut-side down, and cook for one to two minutes or until the sauce begins to become sticky. Turn the bananas over to coat in the sauce. Put the bananas on a heated serving platter and cover using aluminium foil.
3. Return the pan to the heat and meticulously mix in the lime juice and the orange liqueur. Using a long-handled match, ignite the sauce. Allow the flames to die down and then pour the sauce over the bananas.
4. Drizzle the bananas with the toasted coconut and the sesame seeds. Serve instantly.

VIETNAMESE OXTAIL SOUP

Yield: Servings 6–8

INGREDIENTS:

- ¼ cup chopped cilantro
- ½ pound bean sprouts
- 1 (7-ounce) package rice sticks, soaked in hot water until tender and drained
- 1 green onion, trimmed and thinly cut
- 1 small cinnamon stick
- 1 tablespoon vegetable oil
- 1 tablespoon whole black peppercorns
- 1 whole star anise

- 2 garlic cloves, peeled and crushed
- 2 limes, cut into wedges
- 2 medium carrots, peeled and julienned
- 2 medium onions
- 3 tablespoons fish sauce
- 4 (½-inch) pieces ginger, peeled
- 4 serrano chilies, seeded and thinly cut
- 5 pounds meaty oxtails
- Freshly ground black pepper to taste

DIRECTIONS:

1. Cut 1 of the onions into ¼-inch slices. Heat the vegetable oil in a moderate-sized sauté pan on moderate to high heat. Put in the onion slices and sauté until they barely start to brown. Drain the oil from the browned onion and save for later.

2. Slice the rest of the onion into paper-thin slices. Cover using plastic wrap and save for later.

3. Wash the oxtails in cold water and put them in a stock pot. Cover the tails with cold water and bring to its boiling point. Lower the heat and skim any residue that has come to the surface. Let simmer for fifteen minutes.

4. Put in the browned onions, ginger, carrots, cinnamon, star anise, peppercorns, and garlic. Return the stock to a simmer and cook for 6 to 8 hours, putting in water if required.

5. When the broth is done, skim off any additional residue. Take away the oxtails from the pot and allow to cool until easy to handle. Take away the meat from the bones. Position the meat on a platter and decorate it with the cut green onions. Discard the bones.

6. Strain the broth and return to the stove. Put in the fish sauce and black pepper to taste. Keep warm.

7. On a second platter, position the bean sprouts, chopped cilantro, cut chilies, and lime wedges.

8. Bring a pot of water to its boiling point. Plunge the softened rice noodles in the water to heat. Drain.

9. To serve, place a portion of the noodles in each container. Set a tureen of the broth on the table together with the platter of oxtail meat and the platter of accompaniments. Let your guests serve themselves.

VIETNAMESE PORK STICKS

Yield: Servings 6

INGREDIENTS:

For the pork:

- ¼ teaspoon Chinese hot chili oil
- ¼ teaspoon sugar
- ½ cup chopped basil
- ½ cup chopped cilantro
- ½ cup chopped mint
- 1 (½-inch) piece ginger, peeled and minced
- 1 clove garlic, minced
- 1 green onion, trimmed and minced
- 1 pound lean ground pork
- 1 tablespoon soy sauce
- 1¼ teaspoons lemon juice
- 12 bamboo skewers, soaked in water
- 12 Boston or leaf lettuce leaves
- 2 teaspoons vegetable oil
- 6 big water chestnuts, minced
- teaspoon salt

For the dipping sauce:
- ½ cup soy sauce
- 1 (1-inch) piece ginger, minced
- 1 teaspoon oyster sauce
- 2 garlic cloves, minced
- 2 teaspoons sugar
- 3 tablespoons water
- 5 tablespoons lemon juice
- Pinch of cayenne pepper

DIRECTIONS:
1. To prepare the pork: In a big container, use your hands to meticulously mix the ground pork, water chestnuts, garlic, green onion, soy sauce, vegetable oil, lemon juice, ginger, sugar, chili oil, and salt.
2. Split the mixture into 12 portions. Shape each portion into a cylinder about 3 inches by 1 inch. Cautiously insert a bamboo skewer through each cylinder along the length. Set aside.
3. Put the lettuce leaves, cilantro, mint, and basil in 4 separate serving bowls. Place in your fridge until ready to serve.

4. To prepare the dipping sauce: In a small deep cooking pan mix all the sauce ingredients. Bring the mixture to its boiling point on moderate to high heat. Decrease the heat and simmer for five minutes. Take away the sauce from the heat and allow to cool.

5. Prepare a charcoal or gas grill. Put the skewers in a grill basket, ensuring they are tightly held but not squashed. Grill the skewers until the pork is thoroughly cooked and the outside is crunchy, approximately ten to fifteen minutes flipping the basket regularly.

6. To serve, pour each guest some of the dipping sauce into a small individual container. Put the bowls of cilantro, mint, and basil in the center of the table. Put 2 lettuce leaves and 2 pork skewers on each guest's plate.

7. To assemble, have each guest slide the pork from the skewer onto a lettuce leaf. Drizzle the pork with some of the herbs to taste. Roll the lettuce around the pork and dip in the sauce.

SWEET-AND-SOUR CHICKEN

Yield: Servings 4

INGREDIENTS:

- 1 (1-inch) piece of ginger, peeled and minced
- 1 green and 1 red bell pepper, seeded and slice into 1-inch pieces
- 1 pound boneless, skinless chicken breasts, cut into 1-inch cubes
- 1 small onion, thinly cut
- 1 tablespoon vegetable oil
- 1–2 tablespoons prepared chili sauce
- 2 cloves garlic, minced
- 2 tablespoons soy sauce
- 4–6 tablespoons prepared Plum Sauce (Page 34)
- 8 ounces canned pineapple pieces, drained
- Jasmine rice, cooked in accordance with package directions

DIRECTIONS:

1. In a small container, mix the soy sauce, garlic, ginger, and chili sauce. Put in the chicken pieces, stirring to coat. Set aside to marinate for minimum twenty minutes.

2. Heat the oil in a wok or big frying pan on moderate heat. Put in the onion and sauté until translucent, approximately 3 minutes.

3. Put in the chicken mixture and carry on cooking for another three to five minutes.

4. Put in the bell peppers, the pineapple, and plum sauce. Cook for another five minutes or until the chicken is thoroughly cooked.

5. Serve over lots of fluffy Jasmine rice.

TAMARIND STIR-FRIED CHICKEN WITH MUSHROOMS

Yield: Servings 1–2

INGREDIENTS:

- 2 tablespoons vegetable oil
- Salt and freshly ground black pepper
- 1 teaspoon sugar
- 4 ounces domestic mushrooms, cut
- ½ cup cut onions
- 1 clove garlic, minced
- 2 tablespoons Tamarind Concentrate (Page 20)
- 2 tablespoons water
- 1 cup bean sprouts
- 1 small jalapeño, seeded and minced
- ¼ cup chopped basil
- 1–2 whole boneless, skinless chicken breasts, cut into bite-sized cubes

DIRECTIONS:

1. Heat the vegetable oil in a big sauté pan or wok using high heat. Flavour the chicken with the salt, pepper, and sugar.

2. Put in the chicken to the pan and stir-fry for a couple of minutes. Put in the mushrooms, onions, and garlic; carry on cooking for another two to three minutes. Put in the tamarind and water; stir.

3. Put in the rest of the ingredients. Adjust seasonings to taste before you serve.

THAI CASHEW CHICKEN

Yield: Servings 2–4

INGREDIENTS:

- 3 tablespoons vegetable oil
- 1 big whole boneless, skinless chicken breast, cut into fine strips

- 4 green onions, trimmed and slice into 1-inch lengths
- 1 small onion, thinly cut
- ¼ cup chicken broth
- 1 tablespoon oyster sauce
- 1 tablespoon fish sauce
- 2 tablespoons sugar
- ¾ cup whole cashews
- 2–3 teaspoons Chili Tamarind Paste (page 11)
- 5–10 dried Thai chilies
- 5–10 cloves garlic, mashed

DIRECTIONS:

1. In a wok or big frying pan, heat the oil on moderate to high heat until hot.
2. Put in the chilies and stir-fry for a short period of time until they darken in color. Move the chilies to a paper towel to drain; set aside.
3. Put in the garlic to the wok and stir-fry until just starting to turn golden.
4. Increase the heat to high and put in the chicken. Cook while stirring continuously, for roughly one minute.
5. Put in the green onions and onion slices and cook for half a minute.
6. Put in the Chili Tamarind Paste, broth, oyster sauce, fish sauce, and sugar. Continue to stir-fry for 30 more seconds.
7. Put in the reserved chilies and the cashews; stir-fry for 1 more minute or until the chicken is thoroughly cooked and the onions are soft.

THAI GLAZED CHICKEN

Yield: Servings 2–4

INGREDIENTS:

- 1 tablespoon fish sauce
- 1 tablespoon minced cilantro
- 1 teaspoon chopped ginger
- 1 teaspoon salt
- 1 teaspoon white pepper
- 1 whole chicken, cut in half (ask your butcher to do this for you)
- 2 tablespoons coconut milk

- 2 tablespoons rice wine
- 2 tablespoons soy sauce
- 4 cloves garlic, chopped

DIRECTIONS:

1. Wash the chicken under cold water, then pat dry. Trim off any surplus fat or skin. Put the chicken halves in big Ziplock bags.
2. Mix the rest of the ingredients together in a small container until well blended.
3. Pour the marinade into the Ziplock bags, seal closed, and turn until the chicken is uniformly coated with the marinade. Allow the chicken to marinate for thirty minutes to an hour in your fridge.
4. Preheat your oven to 350 degrees.
5. Take away the chicken from the bags and put them breast side up in a roasting pan big enough to hold them easily. (Discard the rest of the marinade.)
6. Roast the chicken for about forty-five minutes.
7. Turn on the broiler and broil for roughly ten minutes or until done.

THAI-STYLE GREEN CURRY CHICKEN

Yield: Servings 4–6

INGREDIENTS:

- ¼ cup (or to taste) chopped cilantro leaves
- ¼ cup Green Curry Paste
- ¼ cup vegetable oil
- 2 cups coconut milk
- 3 tablespoons fish sauce
- 3 whole boneless, skinless chicken breasts, cut into bite-sized pieces
- Steamed white rice

DIRECTIONS:

1. Heat 2 tablespoons of vegetable oil in a big sauté pan or wok on moderate heat. Put in the chicken and sauté until mildly browned on all sizes. Take away the chicken and save for later.
2. Put in the remaining vegetable oil to the sauté pan. Mix in the curry paste and cook for two to three minutes. Put in the coconut milk and carry on cooking for five minutes. Put in the reserved chicken and fish sauce. Decrease the heat and simmer until chicken is soft, fifteen to twenty minutes. Mix in the cilantro.

3. Serve with steamed white rice.

BAKED REDFISH WITH LIME VINAIGRETTE

Yield: Servings 2

INGREDIENTS:

- ¼ teaspoon salt
- ½ teaspoon sugar
- 1 clove garlic, minced
- 2 (6-ounce) redfish fillets, washed and patted dry (skate, sole, or flounder also work well)
- 2 tablespoons lime juice
- 2 tablespoons vegetable oil
- 2 teaspoons soy or fish sauce

DIRECTIONS:

1. Put the fillets in a shallow baking dish.
2. In a small container, mix the garlic, lime juice, soy sauce, sugar, and salt, then whisk in the oil.
3. Pour the vinaigrette over the fish and bake in a 450-degree oven for six to seven minutes or until done to your preference.

QUICK ASIAN-GRILLED FISH

Yield: Servings 4–6

INGREDIENTS:

- 1 tablespoon cut jalapeño chili peppers
- 1 teaspoon freshly ground black pepper
- 1 whole fish, such as sea bass or mackerel, cleaned
- 2 teaspoons brown sugar
- 3 tablespoons chopped garlic, divided
- 3 tablespoons lime juice
- 4 tablespoons chopped cilantro

DIRECTIONS:

1. Swiftly wash the fish under cold water. Pat dry using paper towels. Set the fish on a big sheet of aluminium foil.

2. Put the cilantro, 2 tablespoons of the garlic, and the black pepper in a food processor and process to make a thick paste.

3. Rub the paste all over the fish, both inside and out. Firmly wrap the fish in the foil.

4. To make the sauce, place the rest of the garlic, the lime juice, jalapeño, and brown sugar in a food processor and pulse until blended.

5. Put the fish on a prepared grill and cook for five to six minutes per side or until the flesh appears opaque when pierced using the tip of a knife.

6. Serve the fish with the sauce.

ROASTED SOUTHEAST ASIAN FISH

Yield: Servings 4

INGREDIENTS:

- ¼ cup chopped green onion
- 1 teaspoon salt
- 12 fresh cilantro sprigs
- 3 cloves garlic
- 4 (12-inch-square) pieces of aluminium foil
- 4 (8-ounce) fish fillets (salmon or mackerel are good choices)
- 4 small fresh red chilies, seeded, 2 left whole and 2 julienned
- 4 thin slices of gingerroot
- 8 thin lime slices, cut in half
- Zest of 1 lime

DIRECTIONS:

1. Use a food processor to mix the green onions, garlic, gingerroot, the 2 seeded whole chilies, the lime zest, and salt.

2. Preheat your oven to 450 degrees.

3. Wash the fish under cold water and pat dry. Put each fillet in the middle of a piece of foil. Rub liberally with the green onion paste. Top with the cilantro leaves, lime slices, and julienned chilies. Cover the fish in the foil.

4. Put the fish on a baking sheet and roast for roughly ten minutes per inch of thickness.

5. To serve, place unopened packets on each plate. Let guests unwrap.

SEAFOOD STIR-FRY

Yield: Servings 2–4

INGREDIENTS:

- ¼ cup chopped basil
- 1 can bamboo shoots, washed and drained
- 1 pound fresh shrimp, scallops, or other seafood, cleaned
- 1 stalk lemongrass, bruised
- 2 shallots, chopped
- 3 tablespoons fish sauce
- 3 tablespoons vegetable oil
- 3 teaspoons garlic, chopped
- Pinch of brown sugar
- Rice, cooked in accordance with package directions

DIRECTIONS:

1. Heat the oil in a frying pan or wok using high heat. Put in the garlic, shallots, lemongrass, and basil, and sauté for one to two minutes.
2. Decrease the heat, put in the rest of the ingredients, and stir-fry until the seafood is done to your preference, roughly five minutes.
3. Serve over rice.

SEARED COCONUT SCALLOPS

Yield: Servings 2

INGREDIENTS:

- ¼ teaspoon cayenne
- ½ teaspoon salt
- 1 big egg, beaten
- 10 medium sea scallops, cleaned, washed, and patted dry
- 1½ cups sweetened, flaked coconut
- 2 cups boiling water
- Salt and pepper

DIRECTIONS:

1. Preheat your oven to 350 degrees.

2. Put the coconut in a small container. Pour the boiling water over the coconut, stir, and then drain through a colander. Pat dry.

3. Spread the coconut on a baking sheet and bake for about ten minutes or until golden.

4. Put the toasted coconut in a small container and mix in the cayenne and salt.

5. Flavour the scallops with salt and pepper.

6. Heat a heavy, nonstick pan using high heat until almost smoking.

7. Immerse each scallop in the beaten egg, letting most of the egg drip off, then press the scallops into the coconut mixture.

8. Put the scallops in the pan and sear for one to 1½ minutes per side until just done.

SNAPPER BAKED WITH FISH SAUCE AND GARLIC

Yield: Servings 2

INGREDIENTS:

- ¼ cup fish sauce
- 1 tablespoon sesame oil
- 2 cloves garlic, minced
- 2 whole small red snappers, cleaned but left whole

DIRECTIONS:

1. Using a sharp knife, make 3 deep diagonal slits on each side of the fish. Put the fish in an ovenproof baking dish.

2. Mix the fish sauce, sesame oil, and garlic in a small container. Ladle the mixture over the fish, ensuring it goes into the slits. Allow the fish to sit at room temperature for half an hour

3. Bake the fish in a 425-degree oven for thirty minutes or until the skin is crunchy.

STEAMED MUSSELS WITH LEMONGRASS

Yield: Servings 2–4

INGREDIENTS:

- 1 serrano chili
- 2 pounds mussels, cleaned
- 2 stalks lemongrass, outer leaves removed and discarded, inner portion bruised

- 3 (½-inch) slices unpeeled ginger

- 3 cups water

- 5 cloves garlic

- Peel of 1 lime

- Tabasco to taste

DIRECTIONS:

1. Put the water, lemongrass, lime, garlic, and ginger in a pot big enough to hold all of the mussels. Bring to its boiling point, reduce heat, and allow to simmer for five minutes.
2. Bring the liquid back to its boiling point and put in the mussels; cover and allow to steam for five minutes, shaking the pan every so frequently.
3. Move the mussels to a serving platter, discarding any mussels that have not opened.
4. Put in the chili pepper to the broth and simmer for another two minutes. Strain the broth, then pour over the mussels.
5. Serve the mussels with Tabasco on the side.

STEAMED RED SNAPPER

Yield: Servings 4

INGREDIENTS:

- 1 recipe Thai Sauce of your choice
- 1 whole red snapper (about 2 pounds), cleaned, but left whole
- Vegetable oil

DIRECTIONS:

1. Swiftly wash the fish under cold water. Pat dry using paper towels. Using a sharp knife, deeply score the fish three to 4 times on each side.
2. Fill the base of a tiered steamer full of water. Bring the water to its boiling point.
3. Meanwhile, lightly coat the steamer rack with vegetable oil. Put the fish on the rack.
4. Put the rack over the boiling water, cover, and allow to steam for ten to twelve minutes, until the flesh of the fish appears opaque when pierced using a knife.
5. Serve the sauce on the side.

STIR-FRIED SHRIMP AND GREEN BEANS

Yield: Servings 2–3

INGREDIENTS:

- ½ cup cleaned shrimp
- 1 tablespoon Red Curry Paste (Page 17)
- 1 tablespoon vegetable oil
- 1½ cups green beans, trimmed and slice into 1-inch lengths
- 2 teaspoons fish sauce
- 2 teaspoons sugar

DIRECTIONS:

1. Heat the vegetable oil on moderate heat. Mix in the curry paste and cook for a minute to release the fragrance.
2. Put in the shrimp and the green beans at the same time, and stir-fry until the shrimp become opaque. (The green beans will still be fairly crunchy. If you prefer your beans softer, cook an additional minute.)
3. Put in the fish sauce and the sugar; stir until blended.
4. Serve instantly with rice.

ASIAN GRILLED VEGETABLES

Yield: Servings 6

INGREDIENTS:

- 1 recipe Asian Marinade
- 1 summer squash, cut into 1-inch slices
- 1 zucchini, cut into 1-inch slices
- 12 whole mushrooms, roughly 1-inch in diameter
- 12 whole pearl onions or 12 (2-inch) pieces of white onion
- 2 bell peppers (red, yellow, or green, in any combination), seeded and slice into two-inch squares

DIRECTIONS:

1. Alternate the vegetables on 6 skewers (soak the skewers in water until tender if using wooden skewers).
2. Put the skewers in a pan big enough to let them lay flat. Pour the marinade over the skewers and allow it to sit for roughly 1 hour.
3. Put the skewers in a mildly oiled grill basket and place on a hot grill. Cook roughly five minutes on each side or until vegetables are done to your preference.

CURRIED GREEN BEANS

Yield: Servings 4–6

INGREDIENTS:

- 1 pound green beans, trimmed Steamed rice
- 2 tablespoons Red Curry Paste (Page 17)
- 2 tablespoons vegetable oil
- 6 cups chicken or vegetable both

DIRECTIONS:

1. In a big deep cooking pan, heat the vegetable oil on moderate to high heat.
2. Put in the curry paste and stir-fry for a minute.
3. Mix in the broth until well blended with the paste. Put in the green beans and bring to a low boil. Cook for fifteen to twenty minutes to reduce the liquid.
4. Lower the heat to sustain a hard simmer and carry on cooking until the beans are very well done.
5. Serve the beans over steamed rice, ladling the sauce over the top.

GINGERED GREEN BEANS

Yield: Servings 2–4

INGREDIENTS:

- ¼ teaspoon salt
- ½ cup coconut milk
- ½ pound green beans, trimmed
- 1 stalk lemongrass, minced (inner soft portion only)
- 1 tablespoon peeled and minced ginger
- 1–3 (to taste) serrano chilies, seeded and minced
- 2 tablespoons vegetable oil

DIRECTIONS:

1. In a moderate-sized-sized deep cooking pan, heat the oil on moderate to high. Mix in the lemongrass, ginger, and chilies; sauté for one to two minutes.
2. Mix in the coconut milk and the salt until well blended.
3. Put in the green beans, raise the heat to high, and cook for about three minutes or until the beans are done to your preference.

GREEN BEANS WITH MACADAMIA NUT SAUCE

Yield: Servings 4–6

INGREDIENTS:

- ½ teaspoon cayenne pepper
- ½ teaspoon ground cumin
- ½-1 teaspoon salt to taste
- 1 bay leaf
- 1 cup coconut milk
- 1 medium onion, chopped
- 1 pound green beans, trimmed
- 1 teaspoon ground coriander
- 2 cloves garlic, chopped
- 2 tablespoons vegetable oil
- 2 tablespoons water
- 4 whole raw macadamia nuts, chopped

DIRECTIONS:

1. Put the onion, macadamia nuts, garlic, vegetable oil, and water in a blender or food processor and process until the desired smoothness is achieved. Move the paste to a small container and mix in the cayenne pepper, coriander, and cumin.
2. In a moderate-sized-sized deep cooking pan, heat the macadamia nut paste, coconut milk, and bay leaf on moderate to high heat. Heat to a simmer, reduce heat, and cook until reduced to half.
3. Mix in the salt. Put in the green beans and continue simmering, stirring once in a while, until the beans are done to your preference, approximately eight to ten minutes. Put in salt to taste if required.

ROASTED ASIAN CAULIFLOWER

Yield: Servings 6–8

INGREDIENTS:

- 1 head cauliflower, broken into florets (cut the florets in half if large)

DIRECTIONS:

1. Put the cauliflower florets in a big Ziplock bag and pour marinade over them; allow to rest in your fridge for four to 6 hours.
2. Preheat your oven to 500 degrees.
3. Put the cauliflower florets in a roasting pan. Roast for roughly fifteen minutes or until soft, turning after seven to eight minutes.